When Good Inter_____ Run
Smack Into Reality

Ten Lessons to Coach Yourself and
Others to Peak Performance

Brian Klemmer

insight
PUBLISHING GROUP

Tulsa, Oklahoma

WHEN GOOD INTENTIONS RUN SMACK INTO REALITY
© 2005 by Brian Klemmer

Published by Insight Publishing Group
8801 S. Yale, Suite 410
Tulsa, OK 74137
918-493-1718

ISBN 1-932503-28-5
Library of Congress catalog card number: 2004109011

Printed in the United States of America

Endorsement

I know Brian Klemmer personally but more importantly from the results he gets. Everyone I know who has been associated with his teachings and insight have been profoundly impacted. His book, *When Good Intentions Run Smack into Reality* will not leave you the way it found you. You will be encouraged and challenged. But even more importantly you will gain practical, hands-on, life-altering ideas. I highly recommend it!

John Mason
Best-selling author, speaker

Contents

Acknowledgements

This book is dedicated to my parents, Ken & Alice Klemmer who were everything a child could want in parents. One of the many things they instilled in me was a desire to read. My thanks to my wife Roma, and our three children Kelly, David, and Krystal for their patience as I pursue our company's mission which included the writing of this book. Thanks to Patrick & Nancy Dean, Steve Hinton, Brian Miller, Diane Beinschroth, Sona Van der Hoop, Roy Dayton, and the many people in our office who have spread the Klemmer & Associates seminars to thousands of people around the world the last ten years. Thanks to Lance Giroux for introducing me to this work in 1975, which opened up a meaningful purpose for my life as well as being a great friend. Thanks to my mentor Tom, who I knew for eight years before he was killed in 1983. He opened up a whole new world to me, believed in me, and challenged me beyond what I thought I could do. Thanks to Brian Mast for the editing and layout of this book and his patience with my changes and demands. Thanks to all our clients who have participated in the K&A Leadership seminars and not only improved their own life, but have been in contribution to others in support of our mission of "**Creating bold, ethical, compassionate leaders who will create a world that works for everyone with no one left out.**" Most importantly, I thank God for the beautiful gift of life and His desire to be a part of our lives.

Introduction

Have you hit a wall? Are there obstacles blocking your path? Are you encountering more challenges than you anticipated? Are you looking for ways to get over, under, or around the obstacles you face? Are you stuck?

If so, then you need answers, answers that come in the form of practical tools that really and truly work.

Honestly speaking:

- **You do not have time for impractical clichés;** *though sometimes true, clichés do nothing to help you over the hurdles you face today.*

- **You do not want to spend any time being criticized for not reaching your desired goals;** *you are hard enough on yourself, you don't need anyone else to add to it.*

- **You do not need to be pumped up with false views of reality;** *you need to be encouraged as you stay on course.*

What you need are tools you can pick up in your hands and use for your benefit. You need practical, encouraging, and challenging tools.

And that is the whole reason for this book!

There are ten lessons, each of which can be applied separately whenever you find yourself stuck.

Lesson #1

What the Facts Really Mean

What does it all mean? Interpreting what you experience or applying meaning to facts is a normal part of life.

Be careful! Are you sure what you have experienced in life really means what you think it means? You might be surprised!

To better understand what you believe things mean, it is important to recognize there are two domains in the world around you. One domain is called "**FACT**" (or Experience) and the other is called "**MEANING**" (or Interpretation).

FACT (Experience)	MEANING (Interpretation)
1.	1.
2.	2.
3.	3.
4.	4.
5.	5.

Because the fastest way to change any belief is through emotion, the best way to really grasp this concept is with an emotional event or experience in your life.

Suppose you lost your job. That is an event or experience; it is a detail that would go in the left box labeled FACT.

At the time you lost your job, you either consciously or unconsciously made some assumptions about yourself or about life. These assumptions or decisions would go in the MEANING box.

You might have decided: "Good things just don't last," or "I'm just not capable," or "Life isn't fair." The possible list of MEANINGS is endless because people who have the same experiences inevitably give it different MEANINGS.

Or suppose your boyfriend or girlfriend does not return your phone call. That is an experience that would go in the FACT box. But what does it mean? Perhaps you concluded: "He doesn't care about me," or "She doesn't like me any more," or "I must not be very important."

The possible list of MEANINGS is clearly endless. Whatever MEANING you choose would go in the MEANING box.

Multiple FACTS, multiple MEANINGS

MEANING #1 — During a presentation years ago, I once asked a man how much he weighed. He was overweight and the expected answer could have been something like, "It's none of your business."

Such an answer would have certainly been okay, but he responded courageously, "I weigh 354 pounds." **His weight was simply a detail that went in the FACT box.**

I then asked him what the FACT meant to him. Without hesitation, he replied, *"People don't accept me."*

MEANING #2 — Later, as the group continued to talk, someone else said, "I'm a business owner and I had over one hundred thousand dollars embezzled from my company." **That went in the FACT box.**

"What MEANING have you given to that FACT?" I asked. His response as a business owner surprised me.

He replied, *"You can't trust people."*

MEANING #3 — Another person explained how both of her parents and one sister had been killed in a car accident. **That went in the FACT box.**

"The MEANING I connected with this FACT," she explained, *"is there cannot be a God."*

What does it all mean?

Are you ready for this? These, and all other FACTS you've put in your FACT box ... **don't mean anything!**

Nothing!
Nada!
Zip!
Zero!

The fact someone is overweight *means nothing*. The fact one hundred thousand dollars was embezzled from a company *means nothing*. The fact an entire family was killed in an accident *means nothing*.

You might be thinking, "Did he just say being overweight, losing money, and having your family killed in an accident are meaningless events?"

No, I'm not being cruel and insensitive and saying these events are meaningless or the pain and hurt do not exist. The pain and hurt are real and belong in the FACT box, *but the FACTS do not have any inherent MEANING in themselves!*

Why do these important facts have no inherent meaning? **Because there are other people who have assigned entirely different meanings to exactly the same fact or experience!** That is just the way it is. Two people will inevitably see things differently, so it is impossible for meaning to be inherent.

Or to say it another way, FACTS do not possess values that have been established, pre-determined, decided, and accepted. For example, suppose you go fishing and catch a five-pound fish. That goes in the FACT box.

> Nobody likes to admit it, but facts have no inherent meaning.

When you brag about your catch and tell me how much it weighed, I'm not going to be thinking, "How much is five pounds? According to his measurements or mine?" There is no question as to the value of five pounds. It is what it is.

Not so, unfortunately, with our experiences. They do not—*and cannot*—automatically equal any given MEANING. The pain and hurt do mean something ... *something different to every person!*

So if you assign MEANING to an experience, be it painful or not, you have just decided in your own mind what that MEANING is. *You made it up!*

Let me repeat that.

You made it up. The MEANING you assigned to your FACT or experience is a figment of your imagination.

The FACT box is still full of things that actually happened to you—there's no changing or denying that—but the MEANING you attached to those experiences is meaningless!

What happens when you assign MEANING

It is our human nature to assign MEANING to what we experience. We are very uncomfortable, even scared, to leave a void where we could, or even should, have assigned MEANING. It is a hole we feel compelled to fill.

There is nothing wrong with feeling like this. It's natural and we all do it, but here is the problem:

> **Once you make any FACT or experience mean something, whether positive or negative, <u>you must recreate more events to support that MEANING</u>.**

You'll understand what I am saying with the following example.

More than thirty-five years ago, a young girl, age eight, wanted a certain ten dollar doll very, very badly. For whatever the reason, her father refused to buy it for her. That is the story, and **it goes in her FACT box.**

What is interesting is the MEANING she attached to the experience. Instead of putting "Dad doesn't love me" or "We are poor" in her MEANING box, her subconscious mind chose "I'm not worth it" as the true MEANING.

Her subconscious mind might have reasoned like this: "If I was worth anything, Dad would buy the ten dollar doll, but because he didn't buy it, I must not be worth very much."

When I met this woman, she was almost forty-five years old, had been married and divorced three times, and had a horrible view of her self. You could have put her in a room of one hundred men, ninety-nine of whom were caring, responsible men of character and integrity (I know some of you reading this don't think there are that many good men out there, but bear with me), and she would have gravitated toward the one rotten son of a gun.

> **Who would this woman coincidentally sit down next to?**
> *The rotten son of a gun.*

> **Who would she have a conversation with?**
> *The rotten son of a gun.*

> **Who would she end up marrying?**
> *The rotten son of a gun.*

> **Who does she end up divorcing?**
> *The rotten son of a gun.*

If by chance she were to sit down next to one of the ninety-nine good guys and he was to treat her like a queen, the obvious MEANING to his actions would be that she is really and truly worth something.

BUT her brain had already chosen the "I'm not worth anything (less than ten dollars)" option. To avoid the impending mental conflict, her brain moves her legs so she avoids the nice guys, sitting her down right next to the one rotten apple in the room. Her brain moves her lips so the words come out such that she has a relationship with the person acting like a jerk.

Now she has an experience (be it a new experience) that *validates* her original belief in her self! She has successfully once again avoided a situation that might have caused her to think, look, or assign MEANING outside of her box.

In other words, anything good that might possibly come her way is shot down long before it has a chance to take place. Her subconscious mind will simply not allow it, all as a result of assigning MEANING.

This principle can be positive just as well as it can be negative, but more people suffer from improper training than from proper training!

Living outside the box

Most people have not separated the two domains of FACT and MEANING. They have actually collapsed the two into one box. As a result, MEANING has become FACT and FACT has become MEANING. They are one in the same.

They do not know *FACT and MEANING are two distinct boxes.*

Have you ever seen the 9-Dot-Test?[1] Beginning with one dot, draw four straight lines without lifting your pencil off the paper to connect all the dots.

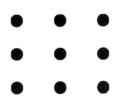

1. The answer to this 9-Dot-Test is at the end of this chapter.

Usually, one or two dots are left unconnected after the four lines are drawn. That is because people are staying within the imaginary box parameters just outside of the nine dots. They assume: **don't go outside the parameters, don't bend the paper, don't rip the paper, etc.**

As a result, their unsuccessful answers look like these:

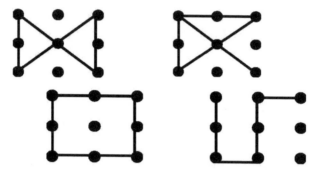

When you assume FACTS have MEANING, like these simple assumptions about drawing a line, you box yourself in, you limit your ability to see things clearly, and you limit your creativity to solve problems.

Like this test, separating the FACT box from the MEANING box will do wonders in freeing you from experiences that have been weighing you down. And since the MEANING you attached to certain "meaningful" events is really irrelevant, how much control over your future are you going to take back?

However traumatic your past, let it go! Imagine the benefit and freedom!

How to reassign MEANING

In my era growing up, a tattoo meant someone drank, smoked, did drugs, cussed, hardly contributed to society, and slept around. It personified everything bad imaginable. But when my boys asked me if they could get a tattoo, my assigned MEANING for tattoos had to change!

I told my boys they would have to wait until they turned eighteen, so when they turned eighteen, they went and got their desired tattoos. I, on the other hand, was busy reassigning MEANING to those who wore tattoos.

It is possible to reassign new MEANING to FACTS or experiences, but it will take some time and effort to reprogram your brain. Here, step by step, is how you do it.

STEP #1
— Admit you made up the MEANING.

And if you made up the MEANING the first time, what can you do now? Exactly! You can make it mean something else.

STEP #2
— Make it mean something else.

And if you are going to make it mean something, then at least make it mean something that helps you instead of something that sabotages your life.

For example, when my children were younger, they would have career days at their school where parents would tell what they did. From airline pilots to restaurant managers and from mothers to lawyers, we had it all. Explaining what I did in my leadership development company was a little harder for them to compartmentalize.

I would play a visualization and picture game with them. In a matter of five minutes, they would memorize the first thirteen colonies in the order they signed the constitution. It was fun and everyone had a good time.

Then I would ask several students (the teacher had privately told me who was flunking out) to stand up and give me the first thirteen colonies in the order they signed the constitution. The "flunking" students always got it right.

"You are obviously a genius," I would say.

You could see in their eyes that their brain was short-circuiting. The experience they were having was not computing with their prior MEANING. Their MEANING box was full of "I'm stupid" or "I'm a failure in school." These MEANINGS they had attached to experiences in their FACT box, such as, only getting four out of ten answers right on a test.

"Now, I'm going to toughen up the test," I'd explain. "Which colony signed after Pennsylvania?" *They would get it right.*

"Which colony signed after New York?" *They would get it right.*

Months later, often these children who had been flunking out would be getting C's or B's. I even had some come up to me a year later and say, "Mr. Klemmer, let me give you the thirteen colonies. I'm a genius!"

STEP #3
— Give the new MEANING emotional value and repeat the new MEANING until you believe it.

The combination of emotion with repetition will help your new MEANING become a "reality." Repetition by itself is seldom sufficient to change a belief system. The subconscious mind is set in its ways. **However, add in emotion and things can change quickly!**

For example, an overweight person who doesn't eat or exercise properly, who has a heart attack, might *instantly* change eating and exercise habits that have been in place for decades. **Life or death is indeed a great emotional motivator!**

> **The more emotional involvement, the less repetition you need.**

Of course, there are always people who will experience something life-altering emotionally, such as a heart attack, and will return to their old habits. For them, the genuine desire to change was not there, so the initial emotional experience wore off and they reverted back.

The challenge, of course, is creating your own emotional experience that supports your desired reality. Unfortunately, there is no easy way to do that. You do know your desired outcome, so work to attain it. Set up an emotional experience that will confirm the reality you want.

When I was encouraging the little "geniuses" in my children's class, my desired reality was for the students to believe they were geniuses. The emotional experience— *standing in front of the entire class and getting the answers right*—was a new experience. It violated their "you're a failure" or "you're stupid" belief system. **For some of those kids the change was instant!**

Once the old belief system is cracked, things begin to change. These "geniuses," for example, will start to hear the teacher differently, they will work differently, they will take tests differently, and they will act differently. All because of a change in their MEANING box.

That some of those students suddenly believed they were geniuses with one experience clearly demonstrates the power of emotional experiences. Most of us, however, need more than one experience to change our beliefs.

We must repeat the emotional experience until we reach our goal. This is why it is critical to meet different people, to put yourself in different situations, to read new books, and to do what is uncomfortable. If you stay where you are and do what you've always done, you limit your growth.

You can also turn up the emotional factor by taking risks, which again has you outside the comfort zone. Here are a few examples:

- **Trouble losing weight**: tell someone you do not want to disappoint that you intend to lose ten pounds!

- **Indecisive about a new home**: write a check for ten thousand dollars to a friend and then say, "If I don't buy a new house within the next three months, you can cash this check."

- **Procrastinating about starting your book**: presell your not-yet-written book.

- **Hate talking in public**: take a class requiring you to speak in front of a group.

Whatever belief system that you want to break out of — and break into — use the power of emotional involvement to "turn up" the heat. Then repeat what you have done until you believe it.

Your new reality

That those young students were able to memorize the thirteen colonies in the correct order goes into their FACT boxes.

What does their successful experience really mean? As you know, nothing whatsoever.

Does it mean they are geniuses? No.

However, I will let them — *even encourage them* — assign the MEANING "I am a genius" to the experience.

Why? Because the MEANING works for their life and will help them much more than the opposite "I am stupid" or "I am a failure at school" MEANING.

When those children reach adulthood, if the "I am a genius" MEANING has been allowed to grow, they will be enjoying the fruit of an orchard planted with little positive seeds many years earlier.

Sure, at the foundational level their attached MEANING is meaningless, as it is with everyone, but since it's their reality, why shouldn't they live the reality they want and need.

That works during their youth. As adults, they would learn at a whole new level that facts inherently don't mean anything. This would be important because they might spend their entire adulthood earning money to be secure. Can you see how a lot of money belongs in the FACT box and does not mean they are secure?

I've known people with millions of dollars who are insecure. So this FACT-MEANING lesson applies at many levels.
You know what that means!

Since **you can define your own MEANING to what you experience,** you might as well live the reality you want as well!

Answer to 9-Dot-Test

By drawing outside of the box and without lifting your pencil off the paper, connecting the dots with four straight lines is easy, as the answer below shows.

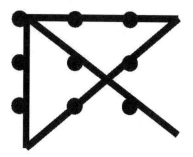

Facts have no inherent meaning! In the freedom that this principle brings, don't forget that facts and experiences will always have consequences.

Lesson #2

Why Problems Are Your Best Friends

A dog is not your best friend. **Your best friend is the very problem you are facing!**

How does the average person think about problems, positively or negatively? Without question, the average person is negative about problems. People view problems from the standpoint of the problems being "bad," "unwanted," "undeserved," and all around, things to avoid.

Maybe this is one reason why they are average!

Average people think a certain way, while successful people think a different way. They do not see things in the same light. The century-old principle stating, "As a man thinketh in his heart, so is he," is certainly true in this case.

While average people are thinking negatively about their problems, successful people view their problems positively. They love problems. **They eat them for breakfast!**

Why? Because problems create value, and the more problems you can solve, the more valuable you will be, the more money you will make, and the more responsibility you will have.

If, for example, you are in real estate sales and the only houses you can sell are the same houses everyone can sell and you can only sell them to the clients everyone else can sell to, then you make the same amount of money everyone else makes.

However, if you can solve problems and sell houses no one else can sell, or sell to clients others cannot sell to, or arrange deals nobody else even thought of, then you can make an enormous amount of money.

> **Problems create value ... *and opportunity!***

But average people sit around and whine about their problems ... not realizing success is staring them in the face!

Slay your Goliath!

Remember the story of David and Goliath? David, the little shepherd boy from out of nowhere, comes in and kills the #1 bad guy, routing the enemy and bringing unexpected victory. The fact is, Goliath was the best thing to have ever happened to David, for without Goliath, David could not have become king.

Today, people want to be king or queen in their respective situations, *but they cannot become king or queen without first killing a Goliath.* That is why your problems are your best friends. They help you reach your goals, moving beyond what you could do in the power or knowledge you now possess.

It comes down to how you handle the problems in front of you.

Four different ways to handle problems

As you have no doubt experienced, problems seem to materialize out of thin air as soon as you set your mind on something. Perhaps problems hide in the shadows, waiting for someone brave enough to start reaching toward a goal.

But now, because you know problems are your best friends, *you have to decide for yourself if that is a good thing or a bad thing.* How you respond to problems will define not only the result, it will define you!

Here are four different ways to handle problems, based on the four different ways people think:

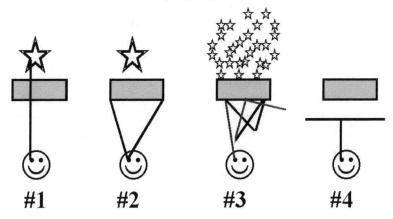

#1   **#2**   **#3**   **#4**

The smiley faces represent you and me, the stars represent our goals, the boxes represent the obstacles between us and our goals.

#4 Thinkers

At first glance, everyone is quick to note the **#4 Thinkers** have no goals. We all know people like this. They are apathetic, they aren't going anywhere, and they are stuck in a rut (You know what a rut is: a grave with the ends knocked out!).

As a result of their thinking, they never run into any problems. They will even tell you with pride, "I don't have any problems."

You and I know that once you set a goal, you will have prob-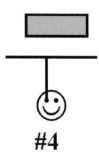lems, but **#4 Thinkers** avoid problems by not having any goals. Consequently, they aren't going in any specific direction. They don't live a whole year; they just live the same day 365 times. They go to work the same way every day, they eat in the same places, they meet with the same friends, and they maintain the same ways of thinking.

If you were to give **#4 Thinkers** the remote control to a TV, they would turn it on, sit in a comfortable chair, and never change channels. What would be the point? They aren't looking for anything in particular, and eventually they would fall asleep. A loud commercial might jolt them awake, but their subconscious mind, which is accustomed to being zoned out, would lull them back to sleep.

Even when **#4 Thinkers** are awake, they are zoned out. Their favorite phrase is, "Huh?" You ask them something and it is almost as if you've jarred them awake, but they quickly go back to their comatose condition.

#3 Thinkers

On the other hand, **#3 Thinkers** don't have just one goal, but thousands of goals! They are very energetic and enthusiastic. Their difficulty is that as they go after one goal and meet resistance, their solution is to simply change goals.

They have many things they are excited about so they simply go after something else. **They are mentally undisciplined.** These are the people you talk to who are "perpetual students," studying to be a doctor one year, then a lawyer the next year, then an architect, then thinking about business, etc.

They are constantly switching goals. Although very energetic, they are running around like chickens with their heads cut off. Obviously, they do not achieve their goals.

In a dating relationship, for example, when **#3 Thinkers** have a breakdown in communication or need to deal with a certain issue, they abandon the other person. Instead of trying to work it out, to bring clarity or conclusion to a matter, they simply leave and find someone else to be in relationship with. And when the new relationship becomes difficult, they simply go find another person, and the cycle continues.

Unfortunately for **#3 Thinkers,** unless they change, they will never reach their goals, much less achieve something great. **That is because nobody becomes great without first overcoming great resistance.**

Whether it's in business, athletics, or religion, those who become great have encountered and overcome great resistance. The act of overcoming resistance, whatever form it takes, is the key that will open the door.

What happens if you give a TV remote to **#3 Thinkers**? They would have a split screen television where they could see multiple pictures at the same time, and they would jump from channel to channel. CLICK! CLICK! CLICK! CLICK!

Have you ever ridden in a car with a **#3 Thinker**. With one hand on the steering wheel and one hand on the radio, the **#3 Thinker** bounces from station to station: news, rap, talk radio, country, rock, commercial, etc. And at the end of the dial, the **#3 Thinker** simply starts over!

Because **#3 Thinkers** are addicted to change and are mentally undisciplined, the first sign of resistance or the first sign of boredom will set them off. As a result, their many goals will forever remain out of reach.

#2 Thinkers

Unlike **#3 Thinkers**, **#2 Thinkers** are very focused, but they still do not solve the problems coming between them and their goals.

What **#2 Thinkers** do is focus too much on the problem. These are your problem experts. They not only know all about the problem, but they want to tell you all about the problem. They are so focused on the problem they get stuck in the problem. The more they think about the problem, the bigger it gets.

You will hear, "You have to be realistic," and "You didn't understand the complexity of the problem," a lot from **#2 Thinkers**. They justify their inaction, whether they realize it or not, by focusing on the enormity of the problem in front of them. Eventually, the **#2 Thinkers** actually become the problem.

If you are ever around **#2 Thinkers**, they have a way of sucking the energy right out of you. One of their favorite phrases is, "Yeah, but ...." When you come up with a good idea, the **#2 Thinkers** will jump right in with, "Yeah, that's a good idea, but what about ...?"

Yeah, but ...! Yeah, but ...! Yeah, but ...! Yeah, but ...!

Before too long, you are too tired to continue.

Hand **#2 Thinkers** a TV remote and they would be looking for mistakes in the movies. If they happened to be watching a cowboy show, they would count the shots from a six-gun, look for tire tracks under the wagons, or look for wristwatch tans on the arms of the attacking Indians.

Wherever and whenever, they love to focus on the problems. In a relationship, for example, **#2 Thinkers** will find two things out of one hundred that are not working and grind on those two items until there isn't any relationship left.

#1 Thinkers

Lastly, you have **#1 Thinkers**. They have big problems. That is because the more successful you are, the bigger the problems you will have. The difference is **#1 Thinkers** solve their problems! They keep their eye on the goal and create, change, grow, and learn in order to solve their problems. Whatever it takes to reach their goal, they will do it.

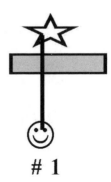

1

They are the creators. They create the televisions that keep the other three **Thinkers** occupied. And when people get bored with televisions, **#1 Thinkers** create VCR's, DVD players, and HDTV. They keep creating and creating.

It is the **#1 Thinkers** who achieve the awards, reach the stars, and achieve greatness.

What about you?

At any one moment, 90 percent of the people around you are **#2**, **#3**, or **#4 Thinkers**. Only ten percent are solution-oriented **#1 Thinkers**. This average is probably not going to change, but what about you?

Which type of Thinker are you?

The next time, for example, a policy changes within your company, look at where the people are. You will see:

- **#4 Thinkers** — "Oh well, it won't make any difference to me anyway." They will be apathetic because they aren't going anywhere.

- **#3 Thinkers** — "How will it affect us? What do we do about it?" They will run around asking a lot of questions in a constant state of confusion.

- **#2 Thinkers** — "I tried to tell them it wouldn't work, but they wouldn't listen to me." They will find every fault imaginable, pointing out how it will hurt people and where breakdowns will be.

- **#1 Thinkers** — "How do I make the new policy work?" They will be solution oriented. They will also be the first ones to gain the benefits of the new policy in action.

Whatever the situation, if you catch yourself at any moment thinking or acting like a **#2, #3, or #4 Thinker**, then you must choose to be a **#1 Thinker**.

After choosing to change, it is important you are aware of your actions. Use the diagrams of the **Thinkers** to increase your awareness. Then remain committed to your change.

That is how you can become a **#1 Thinker**, which, as you know, is the only way to reach the stars.

> The more problems you can solve, and the more valuable you will be, the more money you will make, and the more responsibility you will have.

Lesson #3

Turning the Ordinary into Extraordinary

Do you want an extraordinary life? **Then you must be willing to make extraordinary agreements ...** *and then keep those extraordinary agreements!*

You might be wondering, "What do agreements have to do with living an extraordinary life?"

Life revolves around agreements:

- where you work depends on agreements

- buying a car is based on agreements

- where and how you bank requires agreements

- relationships are built around agreements

- even the earth must be in agreement with the Creator's plan to rotate around the sun

Both the making and the keeping of agreements play a part in your success.

PART #1—Making big agreements

Consider the size of the agreements you are accustomed to making. Using a scale of 1-10, mentally rate the size of the agreements you are making at work, with your family, and with yourself.

Are they large and expansive or small and limited?

If you are not making huge agreements, then you are sacrificing results for the sake of comfort and looking good. You have made a trade. Although you may look good and feel comfortable because you haven't broken an agreement, you have forfeited huge results. In the end, it's a poor trade.

Think of all the people you know who no longer make New Year's resolutions. Why did they quit? They made those resolutions so many times—*and failed to achieve results*—they just stopped making agreements altogether.

> **Mediocre or average-size agreements do not bring extraordinary results.**

They solved their problem with the wrong answer.

The solution is NOT to stop making agreements, but to learn to keep the agreements they did make.

Unfortunately for most people, the need to be comfortable has become such an addiction that they have settled for a life of insignificance.

PART #2—Keeping big agreements

At one point in my life, I made a commitment to raise $4 million to construct a building. I took on this challenge to honor a major mentor in my life named Tom who had been killed in a plane accident in 1983. Although Tom did not have a college degree himself, one of his dreams was to build a university that would teach practical life skills.

After his death, I decided a fitting tribute would be to build university buildings in his memory where these life skills would be taught. I made an agreement with myself that I would reach this goal; I then made my agreement public.

Since I had never made an agreement in my entire life requiring this level of fundraising, it was very uncomfortable! I had no evidence I could even do it. However, during a twelve-month period, I was able to raise approximately $2 million in cash along with another $2 million in pledges.

Again, it was not my talent at fundraising or my experience in this arena. *It happened because I made a huge agreement* ... an agreement I was able to make because it grew out of the practice of faithfully keeping smaller agreements over the years.

Part of being able to keep agreements, even uncomfortably large ones, *comes from the ability to be comfortable with being uncomfortable*.

Did you catch that?

Those who accept being uncomfortable, and place that above their personal and natural preference to be comfortable, are the ones who accomplish great things.

Admiral Halsey, a famous admiral in World War II, is a great example. At one point, he was ordered to stall the Japanese Navy for a period of twenty-four hours. The enemy had battle ships, aircraft carriers, and destroyers, but the Admiral had only small ships. He understood the importance of his difficult position: if he failed to halt the enemy for the required time, there would be major negative consequences for the United States through the loss of lives, equipment, and strategic position. He also knew the cost of being successful.

When the smoke cleared, Admiral Halsey had actually stalled the Japanese navy for almost thirty-six hours and it became a major turning point for the United States in the Pacific!

However, in this battle, more senior naval officers were killed than in all the rest of World War II battles combined! Many of these officers were classmates of the Admiral. As he was weeping afterwards, an aide attempted to console him by saying, "Sir, they were all great men."

Admiral Halsey replied with what I believe is a classic line from history: **"There are no great men. There are only ordinary people who take on extraordinary challenges."**

In other words, it is not so much talent as the willingness to take on extraordinary challenges that determines either average success or extraordinary success.

Throughout the ages, the selfless acts of heroism by those in the military, fire departments, police departments, rescue units, et cetera have always brought the same response from the heroes who survived: "We were just doing our job."

> **Learn to be comfortable with being uncomfortable!**

When crisis comes, those who have practiced to serve and save will do just that. The extraordinary comes as a result.

The unseen price

Are you paying an unseen price? Do you know the price for not keeping your agreements?

The more you are aware of the prices associated with your broken agreements, the more likely you are to make the right choices and keep your agreements.

For instance, several years ago, I got busy and began to neglect the time agreements I set with one of our senior facilitators, Patrick Dean, an incredible facilitator who runs our advanced leadership and teenage seminars. I had rationalized in my mind that as a busy CEO, I had more important things and priorities to handle. However, after Patrick and I spoke, it was easy to see the correlation between some of the problems our company was experiencing and my casualness about keeping my time agreements with him.

Another example of this is Sally. Sally in this case, shows up at a management meeting ten minutes late. She was on the phone making a sale, and she only missed ten minutes of the meeting. "What's the big deal?" she might be thinking. "The first ten minutes are just chitchat anyway."

> **Change comes when we see that the price of <u>not</u> changing is higher than the price of changing.**

But she is completely missing the hidden costs!

Suppose one of her co-workers now believes because Sally cannot be trusted to show up on time, she cannot be trusted with important information. During the meeting, the co-worker decides to not completely disclose all the particulars of what is going on.

As a result, the CEO, who might not have even noticed Sally step into the meeting late, is now making business decisions without having all the necessary information on the table. Like a pilot attempting to navigate a plane using false instrument readings, the CEO must make his decisions on incomplete or faulty information ... all due to a small, "insignificant" broken agreement!

Discover your personal price

What is your personal price for breaking an agreement? You might be thinking, "Well, it depends on the agreement."

Yes, though true to some degree, you might be surprised to find what the price really is.

On a separate piece of paper, make a complete list of whatever you think is important in life. Your list might look like this one:

WHAT MATTERS IN LIFE

1. Time
2. Family
3. Health
4. Money
5. Friends
6. Peace of mind
7. Security
8. Freedom
9. Love
10. Fun
11. Etc . . .

Now, think of a time when someone broke his or her agreement with you. Where were you? What did they agree to do? How did it affect you?

This might be a little painful, but allow yourself to be uncomfortable so you can think about it.

Who paid a price? You, of course, paid a price and lost certain things. The person who broke the agreement also paid a price. Even people who weren't directly involved paid a price. (For instance, maybe someone heard about what happened and as a result they became more cynical about people. That's a price!)

Now, on a separate piece of paper, make a complete list of the prices that were paid. Your list might look like this:

PRICES PAID WITH BROKEN AGREEMENTS

1. Time
2. Family
3. Health
4. Money
5. Friends
6. Peace of mind
7. Security
8. Freedom
9. Love
10. Fun
11. Etc . . .

Notice the obvious? These two lists are identical.

But didn't you find almost everything on your What Matters in Life list was also on your list of what you lost as a result of broken agreements?

Sadly, what matters most is usually the first thing to go.

When agreements are broken, families are fragmented, friends no longer talk to each other, time and money are spent to repair the damage, the desire to contribute and be of service is lost, joy and the sense of fun is gone, stress harms our health, respect for self and others is hard to find, honor and integrity seem less important, trust is destroyed, and on and on the list could go.

Broken agreements are like dominoes—one tips the next one, and the next, and the next. A friend of mine lost over one million dollars and his parent's entire pension fund all because another person failed to keep a business agreement. **What a domino effect!**

In the end, it costs you almost everything you say matters in life.

Not everyone is aware of this reality, but now you are! Let that truth affect your decision making process.

The remedy

Sally, who arrived ten minutes late for her meeting, could have told her client on the phone, "I have an agreement to be somewhere in a few minutes and I respect all my agreements, including those I make with you. When could we continue this discussion?"

Though Sally is not sure how her client will react, she is smart to examine the prices both ways: she might lose her client or she might have a mad boss.

In the end, Sally will need to decide what price she is willing to pay. The bottom line is she will pay a price to break an agreement, and so will you. Make sure the price you pay is worth it.

This is why we should all be careful when making agreements. The price associated with an agreement changes the decision making process.

Some argue there are "big" and "little" agreements, claiming the "big" agreements must be kept while fudging a bit on the "little" agreements is acceptable.

I like to look at it this way. If you have a balloon of helium and you put a big or a little hole in it, what will happen to the balloon? Either way, it will go flat.

The same applies to agreements. All broken agreements, whether "big" or "little," mean the same thing: **you have broken your word**.

When we don't keep our word, our word no longer has power. **This is a HUGE hidden price for not keeping our word!**

Suppose Bob, an overweight workmate, tells you, "I am going to lose twenty pounds," but you've heard the same statement every year for the past ten years. Do you believe him?

Your subconscious mind probably wants to reply, "Yeah, right! Who are you trying to kid?" but you won't

> **The more you keep your word, the more your subconscious mind will work on your behalf to help you accomplish your goals.**

say it. You probably just nod your head, pat Bob on the

back, and walk away. As expected, he never loses the twenty pounds.

Why don't you believe it?

Because the words coming from his mouth have no power. You've heard him say it before, and because he hasn't kept his word, you don't take him seriously.

Why does Bob not follow through with his agreement?

Because the words coming from his mouth have no power. His subconscious had the same reaction you did—that he wasn't serious. Consequently, his subconscious never went to work. Without the subconscious, you have no power.

Either way, the answer is the same: no power.

The more you keep, honor, and remain committed to your agreements, the more power you will have. The more power you have, the more extraordinary things you will accomplish!

THAT is the remedy!

Do you want an extraordinary life? Then you must be willing to make extraordinary agreements ... *and then keep those extraordinary agreements!*

Lesson #4

Are You Really Listening?

Have you ever wondered why God gave us two ears and one mouth? Some say it's because we are to listen twice as much as we speak.

Whatever the reason, few would argue the most important part of any communication is listening. In real life, however, most of us do a great deal of *hearing* but not much *listening*.

We were taught to listen through two filters:

1) the "I AGREE" filter

2) the "I DISAGREE" filter

Unfortunately, neither of these options work!

When the other person speaks, we are thinking, "I already know that, and therefore, what you are saying either fits or doesn't fit with what I already know." As a result, *we start and end with what we already know or believe we know*. Nothing has changed in our thinking.

If "to think is to create" is true, then since our thinking hasn't changed, *our results won't change either*. We aren't getting any better. Our marriage isn't improving. Our income isn't increasing. **The answer is to work on becoming a better listener.**

What it means to REALLY listen

When was the last time you heard someone talk, but didn't hear what was being said?

Did you merely hear the words but miss the other clues? Did you not notice the tone of voice? What was the person's posture saying? Did you detect any feelings behind the words?

More often than not, we hear but don't really listen.

To illustrate this truth, I have tested thousands of people with simple listening tests. Without fail, even though I warn them that I'm testing them, they still fail. Their habit of NOT listening is so ingrained in them.

You have the advantage since you are reading rather than listening to the tests, but let's see how you do. Keep in mind the tests get increasingly difficult.

— LISTENING TESTS —

TEST #1

Directions: On a separate piece of paper, write the lowercase form of the letter "I" and dot it. *(Do it now.)*

TEST #2

Directions: There is a pasture with a papa bull, a mama bull, and a baby bull in it. The baby bull is hungry, where will it go to get food? *(Choose.)*

Pasture

Papa Bull - Mama Bull - Baby Bull

TEST #3

Directions: You are a bus driver and drive a bus two miles north before stopping at McDonalds and buying a Big Mac and a Coke. The bus driver returns to the bus accompanied by a small boy, who has been waiting since 8 a.m. with his mother to board the bus.

The bus then continues seven miles east and stops at Wendy's where the driver purchases a cheeseburger and some fries and returns to the bus, this time accompanied by a small girl, whose mother has also been waiting with her since 8 a.m.

The bus continues four miles south and stops at Chic-fil-A to get a chicken sandwich. Here, the bus driver, the small boy, and the small girl all exit the bus.

Now, what is the age of the bus driver? *(Do you know?)*

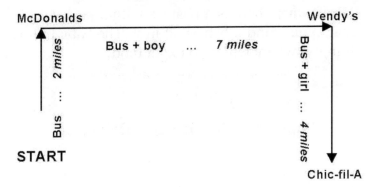

TEST #4

Directions: How many squares do you see in the diagram below? *(Write the number down.)*

— ANSWERS TO LISTENING TESTS —

ANSWER #1

Directions: On a separate piece of paper, write the lowercase form of the letter "I" and dot it.

Result: Most people put "i" on their paper and consider it done.

Answer: A plain "i" is incorrect because the instructions were to write the small letter "I" AND to dot it. So, actually there would be a second dot somewhere above the first one.

ANSWER #2

Directions: There is a pasture with a papa bull, a mama bull, and a baby bull in it. The baby bull is hungry, where will it go to get food?

```
Pasture

Papa Bull - Mama Bull - Baby Bull
```

Result: Most people will naturally think, "Baby needs mama," and say the baby bull should go to mama if it's hungry.

Answer: However, as you know, there is no such thing as a mama bull as a bull cannot be a mama! The real answer is therefore: the pasture.

ANSWER #3

Directions: You are a bus driver and drive a bus two miles north before stopping at McDonalds and purchasing a Big Mac and a Coke. The bus driver returns to the bus accompanied by a small boy, who has been waiting since 8 a.m. with his mother to board the bus.

The bus then continues seven miles east and stops at Wendy's where the driver purchases a cheeseburger and some fries and returns to the bus, this time accompanied by a small girl, whose mother has also been waiting with her since 8 a.m.

The bus continues four miles south and stops at Chic-fil-A to get a chicken sandwich. Here, the bus driver, the small boy, and the small girl all exit the bus.

Now, what is the age of the bus driver?

McDonalds		Wendy's
↑	Bus + boy ... 7 miles	
2 miles		Bus + girl ... 4 miles
⋮		⋮
Bus		↓
START		Chic-fil-A

Result: People stare at me like I am crazy! How could they possibly know the age of the bus driver from the information I gave them?

Answer: If you missed it, go back and read the first sentence of Test #3 again … very slowly. Who is the bus driver? You are! Exactly, now what is the age of the bus driver?

ANSWER #4

Directions: How many squares do you see in the diagram below?

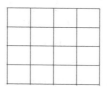

Result: Everyone wants to know the exact number. There could be sixteen squares, there could be seventeen, even twenty-one, or maybe just one. However many squares you see, you are correct.

Answer: The question was, "How many squares do _you_ see?" Whatever number you see, you are correct.

The two steps of effective listening

How did you do on the tests? Reading the tests will, hopefully, produce better results than listening does, but the point is, **the majority of us are hearing but not really listening**!

There must be a way to really listen to people without using the filters, judgment, or comparison we are accustomed to. Thankfully, there is!

To master effective listening, you must understand, and then utilize, the following two steps of effective listening.

STEP #1 — "BEING WITH"

What does "being with" mean? It means **you are present to your own experience and to the experience of the other** *person.* It means your mental nature, physical nature, emotional nature, and spiritual nature are present in the same spot at the same time. You are totally and completely focused on listening to the other person. You are present in the moment.

Let me explain another way.

A golfer is about to hit a ball. Is his mind on the ball if he is simultaneously thinking about the sand trap on the next hole or about what he will say in the winner's circle or about the fact it is Saturday morning and he feels bad about not being at home with his kids?

Is his mind on the ball? He is distracted. He is not "being with" the ball because his focus is somewhere else, and it's likely to ruin his shot. His physical being is with the ball, but his mental being is not with the ball.

It's all part of giving maximum concentration and focus— putting aside all other physical, mental, or emotional thoughts—to the moment when he hits the ball where he wants it.

Have you ever heard the saying, "Never buy a car built on a Friday or a Monday"? That is because cars built on those days are more likely, statistics have shown, to have problems.

The reason? The workers were not "being with" or "being present in the moment" on Fridays or Mondays as they built the car, and consequently, they made more mistakes.

Their physical being was at work, but emotionally they were in the weekend.

When a person is "being with" or "present in the moment," their physical, mental, emotional, and spiritual beings are in the same place at same time. When that is the case, you are increasing your effectiveness – whether you are playing golf or putting cars together.

Similarly, this can also increase your intimacy with other people. For example, when you come home from a frustrating day at work, you are physically at home, but aren't you mentally and emotionally still at work? When this happens, there is very little intimacy with your family members. You might even spend a lot of time with the family, but having a quality relationship is difficult.

> Practice being "in the moment" by paying attention to what you and the other person are experiencing at any given moment.

This same principle applies to sales. For example, if you are learning a script, you are being "with" the script rather than "with" the person you are talking to.

As a result, your prospects feel disconnected from you and don't want to buy whatever it is you are offering them.

Practice being "in the moment" by paying attention to what you and the other person are experiencing at any given moment. Don't judge anything or anyone. Simply reflect from an internal viewpoint, asking yourself, "Why am I feeling this? What is the other person saying, thinking, and feeling?"

In other words, can you tune into the internal dialogue creating the feeling you feel? Continually asking yourself these types of questions will reveal your paradigms, your filters, and your subconscious beliefs … all part of really listening to someone.

STEP #2 — BEING "GROUNDED"

The second step to effective listening requires you to be grounded, which means:

A) you are clear about your purpose and

B) you have removed all distractions.

Can you imagine a surgeon about to operate on you who is still fuming about the argument he had with his wife, the idiot in the car who cut him off on the road, and the fact someone had parked in his reserved parking spot? Would you want to go under the knife with him still muttering how he's going to get even?

His body is with you, but his emotions are not. Your doctor had better become focused or "be with" quickly, or you could be in big trouble!

Similarly, an executive going into an important meeting must become grounded, focused on the tasks at hand, or the meeting will be pretty much a waste of time.

Whatever your situation, get clear about your purpose and remove any distractions. Then, being grounded, you will be able to make quicker decisions, stay on track, respond appropriately, and listen more effectively.

Mixing "being with" and getting "grounded"

In order to properly mix the steps of effective listening, it is important to also understand how we think and interact with others and ourselves on these three levels:

1. THE CONSCIOUS LEVEL
This includes our:

- conscious mind

- head

- five senses

- reason

- logic

2. THE SUBCONSCIOUS LEVEL
This includes our:

- subconscious mind

- heart

- emotions

- memory bank

- autonomic nervous system (runs heart and breathing)

- our five subjective senses (same as in the conscious mind, but at the subconscious level)

- beliefs

- intuition

3. THE SPIRITUAL LEVEL

This includes our:

- connection to God (or if you like, substitute whatever you call the creator or infiniteness)

The fact all of these levels are connected does not reduce the number of barriers between these levels, as this diagram demonstrates:

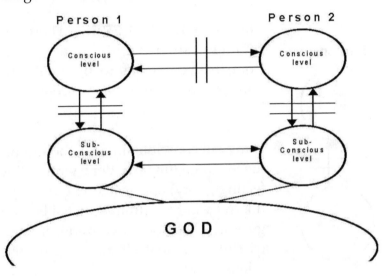

For example, at the **CONSCIOUS LEVEL**, what happens when you and I speak two entirely different languages?

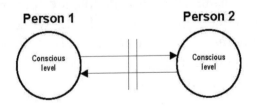

Obviously, there is a barrier between us that we need to find a way to overcome. We have an obstacle at the conscious level of communication.

Or with children these days, does "cool" really mean chilled; does "phat" mean overweight; and does "rude" mean offensive? Again, there is an obstacle in the conscious level of communication.

In addition to language being a barrier to conscious minds, distance can also be a barrier. You living in one city and me living in another city is certainly a barrier that must be overcome if we are to communicate effectively together.

Consider the **SUBCONSCIOUS LEVEL.** There is communication within one person from their conscious to their subconscious and from their subconscious back to their conscious.

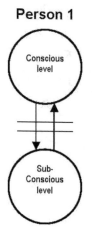

Person 1

Conscious level

Sub-Conscious level

If my subconscious mind is hounding me for something I've done wrong (I'm feeling guilty) and my conscious mind doesn't want to admit it, then a barrier goes up. The conscious mind, in fact, tries to separate itself from the subconscious mind.

Prolonged separation can lead to barriers that might never be overcome, which explains why some people are "out of touch" with their emotions, can do heinous crimes without batting an eye, or choose careers that are not good fits for them. That is a barrier in their internal communication from their conscious to their subconscious.

Similarly, if your beliefs are challenged by what you see with your own eyes, then a barrier goes up if you are not willing to think it through. The conscious mind is speaking, but the subconscious mind isn't listening.

Then when you get to the **SPIRITUAL LEVEL**, there is a constant line of communication between God and our subconscious mind. I have always considered that to be my "conscience" speaking to me, even though it's first received at my subconscious level.

If we turn a deaf ear, both subconsciously and consciously, to what God is saying, the barrier will keep us from hearing. This does not stop Him from speaking, as that line of communication is always there, but we will not be hearing it.

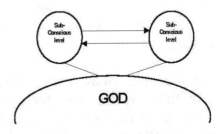

Clearing the barriers

What you've probably noticed from these diagrams is between Person 1 and Person 2, *there are no barriers of communication at the subconscious level.* Heart to heart, two people connect. Language and distance no longer matter.

For example, assuming you and I don't speak the same language, we are blocked at the conscious level. However, at the feeling or heart level, language is not a barrier. If I am frustrated, can you feel my frustration? Yes! Language is not a barrier at the subconscious level. We can share pain, joy, frustration, and beliefs. We are not talking, but we are communicating!

Have you ever had the urge to call someone, and right before you pick up the phone it rings, and that person is on the other line? The subconscious level is not limited by distance.

Unfortunately, the barriers between our subconscious mind and conscious mind usually stop us from listening at the subconscious level. To listen better, both to yourself and to other people, you need to "clear out" the barriers between your own conscious and subconscious levels.

Imagine if you had no barriers. You could communicate perfectly with another person, even if they weren't talking to you!

For example, imagine you have a daughter who does something wrong and feels bad about it. The guilt is causing her to not want to talk to you. A barrier has gone up. What's more, a barrier has gone up between her conscious and subconscious mind as well.

However, now imagine you have done the necessary work within yourself and have removed all internal barriers between your conscious and subconscious. Watch what happens: You (Person 1) can know what is gong on with your daughter (Person 2), even though she hasn't said anything. And on top of it all, she does not even know she is communicating with you!

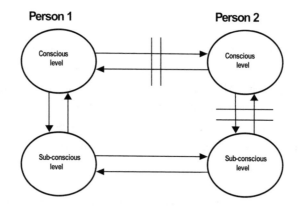

Could you be a better parent if you knew what was going on with your child, even if you two were not

talking to each other? Subconsciously, you can still communicate clearly.

Could you be a better salesperson if you knew, subconscious to subconscious, if your prospect were telling you the truth?

Could you be a better manager if you knew what was going on with your people, even if they did not know themselves?

ABSOLUTELY!

If you know what is going on with other people, regardless of whether or not they tell you, you can be of more service to more people. **That's the name of the game in life: being of service!**

Remove the barriers by beginning to purposefully listen to what your subconscious is saying. (An interactive experiential seminar[2] is the best way to do this.) Be honest with yourself. Deal with past issues. "Come clean" with yourself. That way you have a "clear head," thus allowing your subconscious mind to play its part.

Then you are ready to listen.

Ready to listen

You understand what "being with" means:

> Paying attention to what you and the other person are experiencing at any given moment. You don't judge anything or anyone because once you judge, you can't be present or "be with." All communication stops. Instead, ask yourself, "Why am I feeling this? What is the other person saying, thinking, and feeling?"

2 Go to Klemmer.com/public/personalmastery

You understand what being "grounded" is all about:

> A) you are clear about your purpose

> B) you have removed all distractions

You also understand the barriers exist between the subconscious and conscious levels, and you know how to clear those barriers aside.

What remains?

Listening

Doing it

Taking action

Practicing

Remember, most people do not really listen. But now you understand how to "be with," how to be "grounded," and how to listen barrier-free to your subconscious.

You will be surprised at how much you hear!

Imagine what it is like to listen perfectly!
You can, if you truly learn to listen by "being with" at that moment and by being "grounded."

The Ultimate Sales Formula

Do you have a negative reaction to sales? You shouldn't, because you are in sales.

Have you ever gone on a date?
> That was sales. You either sold the other person to ask you out or you sold that person to say yes.

Have you ever comforted someone?
> That was sales. You were trying to change the way that person felt.

Have you ever convinced your children to be responsible in doing their homework?
> You sold them.

Have you ever been married?
> That was a huge sale. (The biggest problem in most marriages is the same as in most sales – we forget to service what we sold in the first place!)

What is selling? It is communicating in such a way that you cause action.

Most people have sales confused with shoving something down someone's throat. That is not sales. It is stupidity at work, because it never works.

If you want to be successful in anything, selling is arguably THE most important skill to learn.

Since selling is the skill to learn, here is the only sales formula you will ever need:

Want
+ Problem
+ Solution.

Want + Problem +Solution

This three-part sales formula must be applied in this order. Mess with the order and your selling will prove ineffective.

WANT — What do they want?

We are so eager to present what we have to offer we forget to ask our clients, prospects, family, and friends what they really want.

In network marketing, people often commend the virtues of network marketing (making a difference, making a lot of money, creating a residual income, having fun, learning, making friends, et cetera.) without first finding out what the other person really wants or needs.

> This three-part sales formula must be applied in this order.

Consequently, they are ineffective.

In family relationships, we often do the same thing. When my children were younger, I would take them one at a time on trips. On a particular trip to Hawaii with my oldest son, Kelly, I had lined up all kinds of fun things to do. Then I caught myself *and asked what he wanted to do.*

His reply was not what I expected. He said, "I would really like to watch all those action movies Mom doesn't like us to watch."

So instead of going surfing, mountain climbing, or fishing, we stayed in all day and watched six blow-up, blast-'em, action-packed movies. We ordered pizza to the hotel room and had a great time. In fact, *it was one of our fondest memories together.*

I asked him what he wanted to do.

To further prove my point, I told an audience of about seven hundred people to pair up in twos, with one of them holding a one dollar bill. The one dollar bill, I explained, was to represent a year's salary. If either of them lost the dollar bill, they would lose their house! (I wanted them to take it seriously.)

The job of the person without the dollar was to get it; the job of the person with the dollar was to protect it no matter what, and I was going to grade them on

> **"Find a need and fill it."**
> — *Zig Ziglar*

whether they kept or gained the dollar.

You should have seen the place! It was pure pandemonium! People were wrestling, fighting, yelling, screaming, and pulling.

After about twenty seconds, I interrupted the melee. As expected, most of the people without the money did not get it.

"How many of you asked for the one dollar bill?" I requested.

Some had.

Then I asked, "How many of you without the dollar asked the other person what they needed or what you could do for them in exchange for the dollar?"

Virtually nobody had. Those wanting the money simply thought about their own need: getting the money. Those with the money simply thought about their own needs: protecting the money.

When we are knee deep in our own needs, it is easy to forget to ask what other people need or want.

Instead, make it a point to discover what people want and need. Find their wants and needs and fulfill them and you will have more of what you want than you know what you do with.

If you want a pay raise at work, find out what your boss needs, then meet that need. If you want to make more sales, seek to meet the needs of your prospects. If you are a typical male and want more sex with your wife, seek to meet her needs.

As you look to meet the needs of others, you will find some people do not know what they want. Some will even be embarrassed to tell you. You must become an expert "want finder."

The good news is it is easy to practice this skill. If there is resistance, then probe a little bit and assure them of your sincerity. All the while, be sensitive. You want to find their needs, not hurt them to get what you want. Keep their needs as your goals as you proceed.

PROBLEM — *What is keeping them from getting what they want?*

When you have discovered what they want, and they have stated it, *you are ready for them to identify the problems keeping them from getting what they want.*

They *must* be the ones who identify the problems.

You cannot do it. The problems are theirs, and they must identify them from their vantage point. You might very well see their problems, but they are the ones who must describe them to you ... because they are the ones who will be doing the buying.

For example, I've had people who were complaining about not having enough money come right out and say, "The reason is that I've hit the top pay level in my profession."

> **Do not identify the problem ... that is their job.**

If they can't see the problems clearly, you need to be in conversation with them so they actually make a few guesses until they land on what they truly believe is stopping them.

Once they have identified what they want and what their problem is in achieving it, *NOW they are ready for the solution you have been so patiently waiting to tell them.*

SOLUTION — *The answer that will help them overcome their problems and get what they want!*

Step by step, show your client, prospect, or family member how your answer will help them overcome their problems and get what it is they want.

I've talked with people, explaining point by point, why a certain solution is the one they need to follow. It's almost like we are in a room full of doors, and I must help them close every door but one: **the solution door.**

If they are slow at opening the remaining door, then I must raise the temperature in the room, so they have to leave the room. If not, there is the possibility they will become complacent and stay where they are.

When they say, "Yes, that's what I want to do!" then you have sold them! Actually, they sold themselves, but that is what you want them to do. When they sell themselves, it's a long-term sale.

Obviously, all of this is assuming your solution can solve their problem. If it can't, and sometimes in your discussion you will find your solution is not the right solution, then you must tell them the truth. Send them to someone else who might be of further assistance.

Now That You Are in Sales

There is no doubt … *you are in sales.* Whatever it is you sell, remember to use this sales formula in the proper order: need + problem + solution. That is vital to your success.

From there, continue to practice this sales formula until it becomes a natural part of you. It will become second nature to you. Then watch your sales explode!

> The only sales formula you will ever need:
> Want
> + *Problem*
> + *Solution*

Are You Hungry for Feedback?

Are you stuck? *Then go get feedback NOW!* If you aren't stuck, are you growing exponentially? *Then get feedback NOW!*

Feedback should be a constant part of your diet so you **become an expert at giving and receiving feedback.**

How would you rate yourself on **receiving** feedback? How would you rate yourself on **giving** feedback?

Most people are unable to give or receive feedback, so companies pay firms like ours large sums of money to train their people on how to give and receive feedback.

> **You must become an expert at giving and receiving feedback.**

Why? Because feedback is the breakfast of champions! It is the information from which you can make corrections, be more effective, and make timely changes.

Without feedback you are like a pilot flying a plane with no instruments. You can do it, but you are pretty restricted to perfect or near-perfect conditions. The more feedback you have, the more information you can use to make corrections in varying situations and circumstances. Feedback might just save your life! Or your company!

How hungry are you?

If you are going to have an enormous appetite for feedback, you must reduce any resistance you have to receiving feedback. You cannot both want and resist feedback at the same time. You will become a basket case as a result!

Here is how you receive feedback:

#1—Realize feedback is NOT the truth.

Many people are resistant to receiving feedback because they are concerned with it being the truth. They see feedback as gospel and feel they have no choice in the matter. That is not the case. It is simply a person's experience or viewpoint.

If, for example, my son gives me feedback that he doesn't feel loved by me, that certainly doesn't mean I don't love him! **It is his experience, but not the truth.** Since I am interested in a better relationship with him, I want the feedback in order

> Feedback is a person's experience or viewpoint.

to know what I need to do differently so he feels loved.

Sometimes the feedback says more about the giver of the feedback than the one receiving it. Remember that facts do not have any intrinsic meaning? *The same applies to feedback.*

Suppose you are flying and your altimeter says you are at twenty thousand feet. If the instrument is broken, then the truth might be you are at ten thousand feet. Many times you are given feedback from people who are broken, like the broken altimeter.

They have an issue with trust, and so they might give you some feedback you don't trust.

Feedback is not the truth. Again, it is a viewpoint or an experience.

#2—Realize feedback says nothing about you.

Suppose you are still in the plane with the questionable altimeter. If it says you are at twenty thousand feet and you are at ten thousand feet, does that mean you are a bad pilot?

No! The altimeter doesn't care at all about you. It doesn't care whether you are at ten thousand or twenty thousand feet. It merely gives you a viewpoint of where the machine thinks you are.

When you drive your car, how many little adjustments do you make with your steering wheel? Thousands of times, right? Do you realize every time you moved the steering wheel you were responding to feedback that you were off course. How many times were you upset as you moved the steering wheel?

None, which is exactly my point! Your being off course says nothing about you as a person.

#3—Have multiple sources of feedback.

You need to have multiple sources for feedback. A pattern in feedback is more valuable than just one person's input. Widely differing feedback is helpful if you are trying to get a clear picture about what it is you are trying to figure out.

For example, suppose there are three people describing the same book. One might say it is red as they look at the front cover. Another might say it is black and white as they look at the print inside. And another might describe the back cover design as blue. They all have their unique viewpoints, and no one is wrong.

Everyone is right, but it doesn't matter who is right. What matters is everyone is describing the same book. They are three different viewpoints that together give a clear and more complete picture.

Likewise, if three people are giving you differing feedback that gives you a clearer picture of yourself or your situation, then listen.

Learn to give feedback

Learning how to give feedback is just as important as knowing how to receive it. Why? Because in organizations, for example, top management many times will not see the things you see on the ground floor doing the work. Your feedback (experience or viewpoint) is like the pilot having one more gauge to use. But every time you withhold feedback, they are flying with one less gauge, which limits their ability to fly.

Here is how you give feedback:

#1—Focus on making a contribution.

Do not worry about how they perceive you. Focus on making a contribution.

Sadly, most people are hesitant to give feedback because they are concerned others will not like them or will react negatively and take revenge by not being supportive. They sacrifice results in order to be liked.

Others hesitate to give feedback because they feel they are not "expert" enough.

Instead, you should think of feedback as one viewpoint of many and that with many viewpoints the other person will have a more complete picture. If needed, describe your viewpoint toward feedback and ask their permission before you give them feedback.

#2—Be unattached to the reception of your feedback.

You are not trying to convince a person of something. Rather, you are merely offering your viewpoint.

Imagine you are standing on the grassy side of a mountain and I am standing on the rocky side of the mountain. You are not trying to convince me the mountain is grassy; **you are merely offering a viewpoint.** You are telling me what you see.

If I don't want to receive your feedback, you don't need to take it personally. Be unattached after offering the feedback.

A great way to state your feedback is to begin with, "My experience of you when ...." That way it is clear you are not stating what is truth, but are offering your experience or viewpoint.

Another great form of feedback is:

A) What worked from your viewpoint?

B) What didn't work from your viewpoint?

C) What's next?

This eliminates judgment and maintains a forward-moving context.

Get feedback from three select people

Although you want feedback from almost everyone, there are three people in particular you absolutely want to use for feedback. They are: **a coach, a mentor, and an accountability partner.** You want to be proactive and create these individuals in your life if you do not already have them.

A COACH ... *and why you need one*

A coach will help you see your blind spots and will be a great source of feedback ... IF you are diligent in carefully selecting the right coach!

Would you pick a stockbroker without finding out how much he invests in the market and what his track record is? Would you select a doctor without getting references? Would you go to a marriage counselor who had never been married or who had been divorced three times?

Do your homework before you get a coach. What kind of feedback are you looking for? Does the coach have personal experience in this area? Or has the coach just attended a ten-week certification program on coaching?

Not long ago I was holding a Champions Workshop[1] and offered everyone the opportunity to enroll in our Personal Mastery weekend seminar at a discounted rate. A woman came up to me and said, "I can clearly see I need your training to get unstuck, but I cannot afford $395."

I asked what she did. She replied, "I am a life coach."

I was astounded! How could she coach with any integrity if she could not solve a four hundred dollar problem? This is not a coach you would want to solve life problems.

[1.] See "Champions Workshop" on page 125

I am not demeaning the coaching industry. You do need a coach, but you need to do your homework first so you get a coach who has the proper experience you are looking for. In fact, I want a coach who has failed. I was taught to never trust someone who has no failures or who won't be open about them. I want to know how they bounce back from setbacks as I know I will have setbacks along the way.

They do not have to be perfect, but they do need to:

1. Have experience in the field

2. Hold people accountable to standards

3. Set the context by applying all the same things to his/her own life

4. Tell the truth so people can hear and understand it

5. Cause people to win where they would otherwise not win

> A coach is a great system for organized interference.

6. Be a leader who interferes in people's lives and causes them to do what they otherwise would not do toward what matters to you.

Of these six, it is usually the word "interfere" in the last point that scares people. It should do the opposite! Do you remember studying the physicist Sir Isaac Newton? His third law of physics was that a body in motion remains in motion in the same direction until another force comes along.

Ask yourself, what has been the direction of your business? If your business continues on its current path for a year, will you be happy?

Or, what has been the direction of your family life? Will you be satisfied if it maintains its current course for another year?

Coaches can be the force that interferes with the direction your life is taking ... and it is a good thing! A coach can cause you to do what you would not otherwise do, which is a service! (If they interfere for their own purpose or gain, then it is manipulation.)

> **You have to ask if someone wants to be coached.**

Meet regularly with your coach so you can benefit from spaced repetition learning. Depending on your need, you can hire a coach for specific projects or problems and for short durations.

ON BECOMING A COACH

You must know what a person wants before you can be a coach and interfere and be of service. Are you bold enough to interfere?

Whose life can you impact by finding out what they want and then being bold enough to cause them to do what they would not have done on their own? Make sure if you are going to be a coach that you have their permission to coach them.

Are you challenging someone? Is your coach challenging you? This interference is necessary because our belief systems have our behavior on "automatic" to preserve the status quo. Unless you interfere with your belief system, which is where you make most of your decisions, you will recreate the status quo.

Learn to be proactive in interfering with your own life as well as the lives of those you coach. The average person sees the impending results of the status quo and does nothing about it! Instead, get off the wave before it crashes on the shore and go catch a different wave. This applies to companies as well as it does to individuals.

> **Unless you interfere with your belief system, which is where you make most of your decisions, you will recreate the status quo.**

A MENTOR ... *and why you need one*
Unlike a coach, permission is not necessary between you and a mentor. In fact, sometimes, mentors don't know you are modeling yourself after them. You read about them, you watch them, you study them, and yet you may never have a personal conversation with them.

As with a coach, you must do your homework before you think about being mentored. That is because mentors will require you to follow them if you are in a personal relationship with them. Are you willing to follow in their footsteps? Do you respect and value their opinion that much?

It will be worth it because mentorship can super-accelerate your success. Talk to anyone you feel is super successful and most likely they will credit a mentor.

During the '70s, I had a mentor for eight years. I recognize that today:

- I would not be a best-selling author if it were not for him.

- I would not be a Christian if it were not for him.

- I would not be making the difference I am today if it were not for him.

- I would not know what I know if it were not for him.

Interestingly enough, many times a mentor will seek you out because they want to pass on their knowledge and abilities to someone else. They are looking for the right person.

Originally, I went to work for my mentor for the specific purpose of learning how he thought. The job I took and the pay was far below my credentials, *but I was more interested in what I could learn than what I would earn.*

Do you have to work for a mentor? No, but I figured someone more successful than myself would want something in the deal: service. If he had a need, I would seek to fill it. (It's OK to let someone know you want to be mentored, but you must be of service.)

My mentor did not have a job opening for me, so I asked how I could be of service. He gave me one of his problems and I solved it. That was my whole career with him.
Many other people wanted to be mentored by him, but they were stuck on what they wanted. I provided what he wanted: a problem solver.

To have a really effective relationship with a mentor, you surrender to the mentor. Surrender does not mean you give up control of your life because giving up control means you have no choice, but you always have choice. Surrender means totally committing to a choice you have made.

This is why true commitment requires the ability to surrender. You make a choice and totally give yourself to that choice. Average people make a commitment, but never surrender to it. They have one foot on the gas and one foot on the break.

> It is an obligation of a good leader to be a mentor.

Surrender means you trust your choice so completely that you will do whatever is asked of you, even when it does not make sense, as long as it fits your moral code. (Surrender is vitally important and is discussed in much greater detail in the "Heart of the Samurai" seminar[2].)

About two years into working for my mentor, he asked me if I was a leader. What a question! I responded, "You know I am."

He then asked if I was ready. I replied, "Any time, any where."

"Great," He said. "I want you to go home right now and pack your car with clothes. Drive to Eugene, Oregon (an eleven hour drive from where I lived) and check into the Eugene hotel. Then call me. We have a problem. If the situation goes one way, you can drive right back home the following day. If the situation goes another way, you will have to stay and solve the problem. I will explain the problem when you get there; it should take you about two weeks."

2· See page 126 for "Heart of the Samurai"

That was it! I did as I was told and drove eleven hours. The problem required me to stay. In fact, it took me nine months before I went back home! During that time I grew a lot. He trusted me with bigger problems and so our relationship grew.

Looking back, it was worth every minute and ounce of energy I invested. I worked for him until he was killed in a plane accident at the young age of forty-three.

ON BECOMING A MENTOR

If you want to be a mentor, you must first be willing to mentor someone. Once you are willing, the next step is finding someone. Do you take just anyone? Absolutely not! It takes time and it requires vulnerability because you are sharing your knowledge. This is an important decision, so choose wisely.

The truth is, you will not be able to mentor very many people in your lifetime.

AN ACCOUNTABILITY PARTNER ...
and why you need one

Accountability is to accurately account for things. Think of accountants: their job is to track where money comes from and where it goes. They do not necessarily make decisions off of that data (that is the job of the CEO).

Accountants accurately assess where everything came from and where everything goes. This is what telling the truth is all about.

However, few people actually like to be held accountable, which is precisely why we often hear of authority figures being caught in some scandal. And you know if they do not want to be accountable, nobody on down the chain of authority wants to be held accountable.

Usually, the higher you get in an organization, the fewer people there are to hold you accountable. This makes it more imperative to find an accountability partner!

In a study done several years ago of 150 church leaders who had fallen from their positions, they found an interesting common denominator. *Not one of them had a specific person who held them accountable!*

> **"An accountability partner is a truth teller."**
> – Ken Blanchard

If you are going to reach the heights you are capable of reaching, you need both an accountability partner as well as a system in place to ensure that accountability **actually** takes place. (Start with a person and then add a system.)

An accountability partner is someone to whom you can tell anything. You should feel safe and you should be open. It should be someone who is not intimidated by you and who will ask the needed but intrusive questions. This should be someone you actually tell, on a regular basis, whether you are doing what you said you would do, from good to bad.

Many people find an accountability partner in men's and women's groups. Some find it in a spouse. Others find it in a church or business friendship. All you really need is one person. If you are having trouble finding someone, you might try interviewing a few friends to see who would be suitable.

Then agree on a consistent process of reviewing what you said you would do, what you did do, and what you commit to doing. If you believe as I do that, spiritually, there will be a great accounting one day, then this process will be a great rehearsal. If you only get one chance, would you not want to rehearse for the big day? When was the last time you did a physical accounting? Spiritual accounting? Financial accounting?

If you run a department, a team, or a company, start looking for systems that will support individuals in being accountable.

The value of feedback

When it comes right down to it, all of this is about you being the best YOU possible! It is about you becoming everything you are capable of becoming! *And usually, this is much more than you can envision on your own.*

That is the precise reason why you need other people ... and why you need feedback.

Being able to give and receive feedback places you so far ahead of the nearest competitor that you might wonder, "Are we in the same race?"

Your Other Best Friend: Change

Do I have to change?

Good question. No, you do not. You do not have to do anything. But if you are unwilling to change, you will be assuming the *victim* rather than the *victor* position; you will be a car wreck waiting to happen.

Resisting change results in all kinds of problems: fatigue, apathy, stress, and the feeling of being out of control. If you have any of these reoccurring constantly in your life, you will really want to pay attention to this chapter!

Change is not going away. In fact, the need for further change only increases daily! Dealing successfully with change is a critical skill for champions in today's world.

JUST THINK ...

- **Thirty years ago there were no fax machines,** *but they are a necessity for business today!*

- **Fifteen years ago there was no such thing as e-mail,** *yet today, you cannot be in business without e-mail!*

- **Ten years ago, cell phones weighed twenty pounds,** *now they are just ounces!*

- **Fax machines and cell phones were once very expensive,** but now almost everyone has a cell phone and you can get unlimited fax receiving for a few dollars a month!

- **Twenty years ago the cold war with the Soviet Union was the focus of the United States foreign policy,** *yet today there is no Soviet Union!*

- **Twenty-five years ago AIDS did not even exist,** *but 50 percent of some African countries are now infected with the virus!*

An inconceivable amount has happened in the past few decades, and though some are saying the rate of change cannot be managed, the truth is you can manage it.

> **Look around you: growth and cutbacks are both signs of change.**

You MUST manage it!

By managing change, I am saying you must adapt and integrate change into your life in a way that serves you. Use it to forward you toward your vision rather than allow it to beat you up.

Like the tide, there is no way to stop change. And since change cannot be stopped, consider your response to it. Do you want to protect yourself from the tides of change … or do you learn to surf the waves of change?

The question is not whether you will face change, but only HOW you will face the coming change.

Growth or Decay?

One day, Socrates, a mentor to Plato, told Plato that everything went through three stages: *growth, stability,* and *decay.* During the growth stage everything expanded or grew; during the stability stage nothing changed; and during the decay stage things got smaller, eroded, or reverted back to their old condition prior to growth.

Plato, after giving thought to Socrates' statement, developed another viewpoint. Plato determined that stability as a concept did not accurately describe reality. **He believed the world was either in the process of growing or the process of decaying.**

Their differing viewpoints looked something like this:

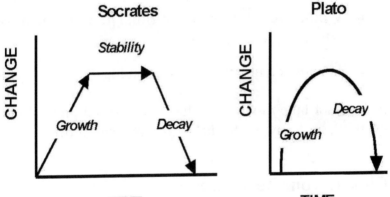

Then Plato boldly stated, **"There is no such thing as stability!"** There is fast growth and slow growth, slow decay and fast decay, but there is no stability.

If there is no such thing as stability, why do so many people believe in it?

Stability does imply safety and comfort, but if stability is nothing but an illusion, then there is no reason to wish for it. Some even consider stability to be a goal that they can attain. Talk about an impossible goal to reach!

Instead of trying to reach stability, a more powerful and meaningful goal would be to **focus on remaining in the growth process**. That way you are always improving and bettering yourself.

If you side with Plato and believe there is no stability, then consider the following:

- If you are married, or in a significant relationship, how is your marriage? Is it growing or decaying?

- How about the state of your physical health?

- Would you say your spiritual development is advancing or regressing?

- Is your career growing or decaying?

It does not take much to realize every situation is either growing or decaying. *Stability is an impossibility.*

Choose Your Response

Since change is a part of the design of the universe, how can we be more effective in our lives knowing this fact and always being in the midst of change? Our great ally in this life is called, "choice." We can choose our response in every situation.

Occasionally we are able to control the speed and direction of change, but not always. If the change is imposed on us, then the only power we have is in how we respond.

In his book, *Man's Search for Meaning*, Viktor Frankl writes of his personal journey and discovery while imprisoned in a Nazi concentration camp. He found that even in the midst

> **We *always* have the ability to control our *response* to change.**

of the most horrible situations, response was still a choice. **That does not mean it is easy, it only means it is possible.**

Have you ever noticed your body's response to fear and excitement is the same? In both cases your heart rate speeds up, your breathing gets faster, and perhaps your palms get sweaty. *The only difference is in how you view what is happening to you.*

Fear is a normal response to any new or unfamiliar situation, but fear is always based on a picture of a negative outcome. If your dominating viewpoint of life is negative, then fear is a bigger factor in your life. If your dominating viewpoint of life is positive, then excitement and anticipation is a bigger part of your life.

Whatever your disposition, fear is a choice. Even if fear is an unconscious, automatic response, it is still a choice. There is always a space in time after an event before you experience anything. It is a small fraction of time during which you can choose fear or excitement.

If you have already chosen fear consciously or unconsciously, you can rechoose the feeling that will work for you: excitement!

You always have the option: fear or excitement.

#1 — Choosing Fear

If your response to change is one of fear, then you will either attack or avoid. This includes getting mad or hiding, lashing out or going to bed, fighting or ignoring the issue, etc. All of them are fear responses.

And what happens **after** you attack or avoid? **Change takes place anyway! It is inevitable!**

#2 — Choosing Excitement

Instead of choosing fear, you can respond with *excitement*, which in turn leads to opportunity and progress.

Take advantage of the change coming your way. Allow it to propel you toward even greater success.

And what happens **after** you choose excitement? **Change takes place anyway! It is inevitable!**

Choose the Consequences You Want

Changes happen both ways, whether you choose fear or excitement. The change will obviously be different, reflected in the quality of your life's experiences and the consequences of your decision.

Will you be the victor or victim?

Will you win or lose?

Will you seize a new opportunity or miss it?

> All our resistance will not stop the process of change.

If you wisely choose excitement, you will have the creativity to find solutions, which will lead to growth and opportunity. When the change comes, you will be glad you chose excitement over fear.

If you choose fear, you will attack or avoid the coming change, which will lead to decay. Then change will come and you will be stuck with the consequences of your choice.

It is up to you. Choose which you want.

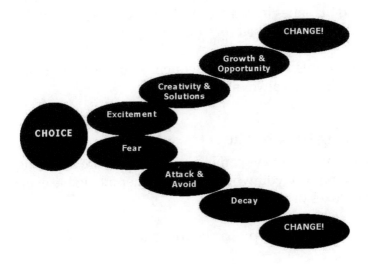

If you find yourself somewhere along the path of fear and recognize you should have chosen excitement, it is possible to flip over to the excitement side.

It is simple, but not easy to do so. The simple part is you are on the wrong side and you need to choose excitement instead of fear. It is not easy because it will require you to consciously choose excitement over fear. One way to move from fear to excitement is by asking the question, "Where is the opportunity?"

Excitement or fear, the choice is up to you!

After eight years of working for my boss and mentor, he died suddenly in a plane accident. Change was instant in the company, to say the least! Some of employees reacted with fear, wondering: "What will happen to our jobs?" or "I'll wait and see what happens," or "It won't be the same without him." Many chose to leave the company.

Other employees, though tremendously sad at his death, began to say: "Where is the opportunity?" or "How can I step into his shoes in this area?" or "Can we creatively find better answers than before?" Business grew as a result.

Our responses, and the consequences of our responses, were choices. It's always a choice!

Preparing for Change

Since change is always coming, you can prepare for change in the same way you would for any other inevitable event, such as taxes or winter.

Here are four tips to preparing for change:

TIP #1 — Create areas in your life that consist of very slow change.

By doing so, you can withstand greater demands of change in other areas of your life. For example, I prefer keeping my physical surrounding, such as my home, very slow to change. This allows other areas in my life to change more quickly without me feeling too "out of control" or pressured.

My mentor's wife used this principle after the death of her husband. She initially made very few role changes in the company in order to cope with the large changes in her personal life: losing her husband and father to her children. What areas of your life do you want rapid change in? What areas of your life can you counter-balance with slow change?

TIP #2 — Practice flexibility

Allow yourself to intentionally and actively try new ways of doing the unfamiliar. Let a co-worker or family member take the lead when normally your way would be the norm. When plans change unexpectedly, instead of becoming stressed out, take a deep breath and "go with the flow." Who knows, perhaps you'll enjoy the new way!

TIP #3 — Develop the art of surrender

Instead of automatically reacting with resistance when change comes, practice the art of surrender. Sometimes it is just best to "give way" and learn to adjust.

Surrender is appropriate during those times when change is not a violation of your principles, when it proves to be a quicker route to your goals, and is basically part of events that "just happen" in day-to-day life.

I find when I relax and surrender in certain situations, things actually turn out better than if I had forced my own way or plan. Also, some things are just not important. Let the little ones go so you can focus or prepare for the big ones.

TIP #4 — Develop your spiritual relationship

Almost without exception, those who accomplish great things have a strong spiritual component to their life. It is like a stabilizer in a world where stability is not possible. If you view God as infinite, **it puts any unwanted finite change in perspective.**

Personally, being spiritually grounded has seen me through many changes I otherwise would have seen as insurmountable.

Evaluate the Change

You control your response to change, so take a moment and evaluate the change coming your way. Ask tough questions.

ASK: "DO I NEED A WHOLE NEW BOAT, OR DO I JUST NEED TO ADJUST THE SAILS?"

While North America was being settled and modernized, the changes taking place were dramatic, permanent, and unstoppable. From the gun to the railroad and from the telegraph to the car, those who didn't submit to the change were left behind in one way or another. Changes like these require you to get a new boat!

Have you ever seen a company come up with a great product or service, do phenomenally well, expand, then crash and burn? They are like a ship at sea that runs right into land!

Instead, adjust your sails if necessary (by responding with excitement, looking for opportunity, being creative, and looking for solutions) so you can stay on course toward your goals.

ASK: "AM I BEING ASKED TO CHANGE MY PRIN-CIPLES OR MY STRATEGY?"

It is okay to modify your strategies to manage change, but not your principles. Principles like honor, trust, taking responsibility, integrity, et cetera are not to be modified. They represent who you are.

That is why it is important for you to know what you believe in, as your beliefs will affect how you deal with change. Unfortunately, most people have failed to make a conscious

> **Ride the wave ... *but get off before it crashes on the***

decision about what they believe and this vagueness and uncertainty robs them of not only clarity but also *power*.

There is not ONE set of values you should adopt. It is a question of examining your own life and making a determination of what principles you wish to embrace simply because these principles reflect what your life is all about.

Then when you are faced with challenges, though you may not know all the intricate complexities, *you can always measure those details against whether they match your principles*. You now have solid ground on which to stand no matter the circumstance.

Sometime after the death of my mentor, I had a career decision to make. The new owner of the company decided to eliminate all seminars taught on foreign soil and to focus entirely on cities in the United States. They felt the focus would increase not only the overall profitability of the company but would actually increase the number of lives we were touching.

I did not like this change, as I was doing seminars in the Philippines at the time and was attached to many of the people there, but in examining this change I decided it did not conflict with my values or principles. It was a "strategy" change, and though I did not like it, I got on board and became a supporter of the effort.

Later on, this same new management team directed me to stop using the word "God" in my seminars. In their mind, it was a strategy change, but this conflicted with my values and principles. Not only do I view myself as a spiritual being, but I hold the spiritual aspect to be a critical part of my seminars (not teaching religious dogma, but advocating a spiritual component for success in life).

I refused to compromise and was willing to lose my job over it. Needless to say, it caused a lot of conflict, but I kept my job. I eventually left the company because of other divergent principles. My stand on principle opened up many doors and allowed me to affect many more people.

ASK: "WILL YOU REMEMBER THIS CHANGE IN FIVE YEARS?"

It is always good to put the change you are facing in perspective. Is it going to affect you five years from now?

Look at the risk versus rewards ratio by changing or not changing. If it is important, then change. If you are not even going to remember it five years from now, then save your energy and focus on something else!

When All Is Said and Done

Are you handling change or is change handling you? *Are you more like a carrot, an egg, or coffee?*

Consider the following before you answer:

- **Add boiling water to a carrot** … and you end up with a limp, squishy vegetable.

- **Add boiling water to an egg** … and the soft inside turns hard.

- **Add boiling water to coffee** … *and it changes the water completely!*

What challenges have you been experiencing in your career, family life, physical health, or spiritual growth? Think of any of those situations as the boiling water.

Some people are like carrots. They act tough, but when the challenges of life soften them, they wilt and refuse to stand up for themselves.

Other people are like eggs. As they confront challenges, they become hard and calloused on the inside and cease to connect and relate to people.

You should be like coffee. When changes and challenges come your way, you actually change the situation! You ride the wave! You find the opportunity in the change and make it work for you!

Choose change … *because it's coming!*

The question is not whether you will face change … *but only HOW you will face the coming change.*

The Secret Path to Better Results: Context

Every day you are experiencing the results, either positive or negative, of the environment that you have created.

A specific environment will give birth to specific results. That is because you cannot experience results in conflict with their environment. In other words, once you create a certain environment, you have set in motion the results to follow.

> **You cannot experience results that are in conflict with their environment.**

Unfortunately, most people try to create results by a direct approach. They attempt to force a change rather than create an environment where the change will inevitably take place.

What context has to do with it

Have you ever heard someone say, "You have taken that out of context"?

What do they mean by context? Context is the environment surrounding something. If you take something out of context, you have changed the meaning of the content.

Suppose I have a jar of jellybeans. The jar represents the context and the jellybeans represent the content. If I change the context from a clean glass jar to a soiled garbage can, then I have changed the jellybeans (content) from edible to inedible.

By changing the context, the jellybeans changed, at least in our perception.

Have you ever been in a group of people and been asked to share something you did not want to reveal? Perhaps it was too personal or too embarrassing. From your perspective, they had no right to know and you did not feel comfortable revealing yourself.

Your response was entirely normal, but if several of the group leaders stood up first and shared the same information requested of you, would that not change things? And if what the leaders said was more personal or more embarrassing than what you would have said, you would not feel under much pressure at all. If enough people are participating, you might even enjoy telling about yourself!

> **In terms of producing results, context is everything!**

In both scenarios, what was requested of you did not change. The only difference was the context or environment of the group. As a result, what you felt comfortable sharing was consistent with the established context.

In terms of producing results, context has everything to do with it!

Set the context to get the results you want

To get the results you want, you must consciously set the right context for your business, your relationships, and any other area of life. **If you do not intentionally set the context, it will be set by default, and people's actions, attitudes, and results will come from that context.**

This is precisely how selfish, nonethical executives can influence entire companies. Not all of the employees could possibly share the same self-centered outlook, but that context produces those exact same results.

In an effort to set the context of an organization, leaders have gone to great lengths to create "value" statements and "mission" statements. (A value statement is a list of values the organization desires to operate by in achieving their goals and the mission statement refers to what they are actually trying to accomplish.)

Though these statements can be beneficial, they **declare** the context but do not **set** the context. That is why the actual culture of an organization can be vastly different from what they have declared in their value and mission statements.

To get the results you want, you must first set the appropriate context. Here is how you do it:

STEP #1—identify the result

The first step in getting the results you want is to clearly identify the results you want. It might sound simplistic, but you must first define what it is you really want.

If you want prosperity, health, closeness to God, or a great parent-child relationship, write it down. Make your list as long or as short as you want it to be.

STEP #2—identify the context and the pieces of that context

The second step in getting the results you want is to clearly identify the context that will provide you with the results you want. For example, if you want to double your income, a context of prosperity is necessary.

Every context is made up of many smaller pieces, much like the pieces of glass in a stained glass window. A context of prosperity would include a giving context, opportunity versus problem context, long-term versus short-term context, abundance context, self-control context, and more.

Write down all the pieces of context that you need to get the results you want.

STEP #3—rate your current contexts

On your list you now have the results you want, the matching contexts you need, and a list of the corresponding pieces of each context.

The third step in getting the results you want is to rate your current contexts. If, for example, doubling your income is one goal and you wrote down "self-control" and "risk taking" as two of the contexts needed, then the third step is to rate your current contexts for self-control and risk taking.

Let's suppose your list of pieces of contexts under prosperity looked like this:

Giving	1 2 3 4 5 6 7 8 9 10
Self-control	1 2 3 4 5 6 7 8 9 10
Abundance	1 2 3 4 5 6 7 8 9 10
Opportunity	1 2 3 4 5 6 7 8 9 10
Boldness	1 2 3 4 5 6 7 8 9 10
Risk taking	1 2 3 4 5 6 7 8 9 10
Long-term thinking	1 2 3 4 5 6 7 8 9 10

Rate yourself from 1-10 (1 equals terrible and 10 equals perfect) on how you are **currently** displaying the contexts that will give you the results you want.

Your honest evaluation will reveal which areas you need to work on to get your intended results. If you rated a context as a "3," then clearly you are not currently getting the results you want. Increase that context by several points and you will be much closer to your desired result.

STEP #4—get feedback on your context

Without showing anyone how you have rated your own current context, have someone else whose judgment you respect evaluate your context. If the person you select has had success in areas where you need improvement, ask them to share with you what context they set for themselves to gain their good results.

This is an important part of getting the results you want because you may be blind to the correct context you need to set. For instance, when I first went to work for my mentor, I had a zero net worth and was making about two thousand dollars a

> **Ask for feedback from people who have obtained the results you desire.**

month. My mentor, on the other hand, owned a two thousand acre ranch, expensive automobiles, several planes, nice clothes, and jewelry.

I knew my context for abundance was skewed, so I asked his opinion about creating a better context of financial abundance. He encouraged me to restructure my life so that I tithed 10 percent (giving 10 percent of every dollar to wherever I received spiritual nourishment), invested 10 percent, and then lived off the remaining 80 percent .

Married and with two little children, I sold one of our cars and bought an old station wagon. Because I had no car payments, I could give 10 percent to our church and invest 10 percent.

Interestingly, I had someone tell me I must not have an abundance consciousness because I had bought an old station wagon. Instead, this person said, I should spend my money leasing a fancy car, even if it left me unable to tithe. I was smart enough to notice this individual attempting to advise me on a wealth context had no wealth of his own! His context would do me no good!

STEP #5—take action

Once you have chosen the desired results and clarified exactly which areas of context you want to improve, **action is required to set the context firmly in place.**

To set your context, you have four options. Choose whichever works best for you and your situation:

1) **Add to the context**

2) **Remove from the context**

3) **Move the entire context**

4) **Take personal action**

Add to the context:

In my mentor's company there was a period of several years where results were flat and classes seldom got over forty people. We had hit a plateau. As a result, he decided to hire a couple of people from outside the company who had been in much larger organizations.

There was some natural resistance because these individuals did not know "our" way of doing things, but that was precisely the reason for bringing them in! They thought on a grander scale and immediately started to explore ways to increase classes to two hundred!

Many long-standing employees mouthed their agreement to increase the class size, but privately they thought we would lose the intimacy of our forty person classes. They were not open to a solution that might compromise their current situations. All told, they simply wanted things to remain the same. Within the year, we were holding classes for two hundred!

Remove from the context

My mentor once sent me to another city to save a failing seminar market. The registration for our seminars was consistently so small that we were about to close down the office.

When I arrived, I noticed a lot of teenagers were hanging around our office. The environment or context they created was driving away successful business people. Again, context (youthfulness) had created content (lack of business people)!

While the teenagers were fine young people who deserved to be served, they were hurting our more professional market. To remedy this, I created another place for the teenagers to hang out and made it clear they were no longer to meet around our office area.

This changed how we were perceived and what type of people we attracted. Within a short period of time, the area was a thriving market for our seminars. Instead of simply trying to apply more effort to increase the number in our classes, we put effort into changing the context and as a result, the class sizes increased.

Move the entire context

A gentleman named Rance Masheck came to me years ago seeking my counsel. He was being forced to move from his eight hundred dollars a month apartment. Rance had spent some time looking at other apartments and had narrowed it down to two possibilities. He wanted to know from an abundance context which apartment he should choose.

One apartment rented for the same $800 dollars a month as his present apartment and the other rented for $1,200. *Because context is determined by its relationship to something else,* I asked Rance some questions to truly determine the right context for him.

"How do you **feel** in the new eight hundred dollar a month apartment?" I asked. He said he did not feel very good since the neighborhood was run down. However, he was not sure he could afford the more expensive apartment.

"How do you feel in the $1,200 a month apartment?" I then asked. He said he felt luxurious, proud, and inspired!

I told him he could **NOT AFFORD** to live in the cheaper apartment! The less expensive apartment would create a poverty context that would then affect what jobs he sought, how he performed on those jobs, and what he felt worthy of asking for in salary.

Rance took the $1,200 a month apartment and within a matter of two years he had bought a house. Within another year he had bought an entire apartment building. Today, he owns several homes, a yacht, and a plane.

Again, because context is determined by its relationship to something else, other people might have felt "burdened" by the higher payment of $1,200. They would not have felt the same motivation and inspiration Rance experienced. In that case, they could not afford to live in the $1,200 a month apartment because it would have affected them negatively.

Keep in mind that there is a big difference between feeling "burdened" and being uncomfortable. When you are burdened, you are in a depressed state because of a perceived weight, which is an unhealthy situation!

It is, however, okay to feel uncomfortable. **In fact, most newly implemented contexts will initially cause you to feel uncomfortable.**

When I purchased my first jaguar automobile, I felt very uncomfortable. I felt uncomfortable with the payments even though I knew I could handle them. I felt uncomfortable about what my fellow army officers might think of me. I even felt

> **Your context cannot stay what it is today.**

uncomfortable about my choice of dress while driving the jaguar. (I remember going to the beach and wearing pants over my bathing suit because it felt improper to drive a jaguar in a bathing suit!)

Are you willing to be uncomfortable to achieve your desired results? It is all part of moving the entire context to reach your goals.

Take personal action

Not long ago, my daughter took personal action and started a new weight loss program. My wife decided to support her by going on the same program. I looked at them both and said, "I am not going to cook for just myself!" So I joined the same program.

Within two days my daughter had quit and within a week my wife had also quit. However, I was having success, so I stayed with the program!

Although my daughter was unsuccessful with that particular program, her action set the context for a healthy household. Because I continued to stay on the program, it caused my wife and daughter to continue to read and research healthy eating and nutrition. I had set the context that led to another program that they both use successfully.

Although our individual strategies and actions differ somewhat, it all came as a result of an improved context of health. When we took action, the context was set.

What are you waiting for?

Most people will continue to do the same thing over and over and expect different results. **But you know the truth: you will never get different results by doing the same old thing!**

You have to change your context if you want to take your life to the next level of satisfaction and accomplishment.

Take a fresh look at your contexts and begin to notice what you are seeing, hearing, and doing. What magazines, books, and newspapers do you read? What programs do you watch on television? What places do you go to for entertainment? Where do you shop? Who do you spend your time with? What clothes do you wear? What type of speech do you use?

What is the context all these activities and decisions have created? Does your context champion your goals and desires? If not, today is the perfect day to change all that!

What are you waiting for?

You cannot experience results that are in conflict with their environment. That is great news, because it means that the exact opposite holds true!

Are You Playing the Victim-Persecutor-Rescuer Game?

Whether we were aware of it or not, we have all played the Victim-Persecutor-Rescuer game. The **VICTIM** claims some sort of injustice, the **PERSECUTOR** heaps on the abuse, while the **RESCUER** tries to solve the problem for the victim.

Unfortunately, once you enter the game, you are trapped into playing one of the roles:

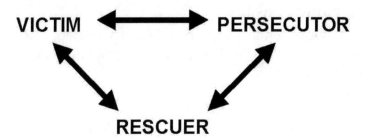

Suppose a husband and wife are getting ready for some function and she pulls a little **VICTIM** attitude by saying, "I just don't have anything to wear."

The husband steps into either the **RESCUER** role or the **PERSECUTOR** role with his reply. If he chooses the **RESCUER** role where he solves the problem for the victim, then he might say, "Well honey, why don't you wear the blue outfit?"

But **VICTIMS** really don't want someone to solve their problems, even though that is what they ask for. She might slip over to the **PERSECUTOR** role, attacking her husband with, "No, dummy, I wore that outfit last week!"

Now the husband moves into the **VICTIM** role, replying, "Oh, you are always picking on me."

She steps into the **RESCUER** role and replies, "There, there, it's OK. I will take care of you."

Now the husband jumps into the **PERSECUTOR** role and says, "Stop doing that! I don't need you to take care of me!"

And on and on the game goes. Talk about confusing!

The game goes on

I own some rental properties. When I started, I would have tenants play the **VICTIM** and complain they could not pay the rent.

Thinking I was being a nice guy, I would be the **RESCUER** and say, "OK, you can slide on the rent for two more weeks."

Then, as their financial problems increased, guess who they would end up blaming for their problems? Me!

They had become the **PERSECUTOR**. I would be the **VICTIM** and complain that you just could not get good tenants these days. And on the game would go.

We have all seen this with children. The child goes **VICTIM** with, "I am only a child, so do this for me, daddy." The parent then swoops in as the **RESCUER** and saves the day (even when the child is thirty-five years old!), then claims the **VICTIM** role when the child acts spoiled. The child can easily slip into the **PERSECUTOR** role by blaming the parent for being too much of a push over. The game never stops.

The game is rampant in business. Suppose several employees go **VICTIM** and come to the boss to solve a problem. Why not? Heck, it makes their job easier, they don't have to think, it takes less time, etc.

The unaware boss, thinking he is doing the right thing, steps in and solves the problem. He pats himself on the back as being a real "doer" and "servant leader." He might be thinking, "Look at me. I am hot stuff. I can solve anything."

His ego is fed for a while, but before long the boss slips into the **VICTIM** role and starts complaining that there just are not enough hours in the

> **Choose responsibility!**

day to get everything done. Of course there are not enough hours when he is doing twenty other people's jobs. The game goes on.

Avoid the trap!

The only way out of the game is for someone to choose to be responsible and cause the other person to be responsible as well.

When you see the game being played from any role, consciously avoid stepping into any of the remaining roles. Choose to be responsible.

Responsible: the viewpoint where you are "at cause" for your experience out of the choice or choices you have made.

In other words:

- Do not solve other people's problems by stepping into the **RESCUER** role.

- Do not play the **VICTIM**.

- Do not allow a **PERSECUTOR** to push you into the game.

This is not an excuse to be cold and uncaring. **Be caring enough to believe others capable of solving their own problems and support them in them solving the problem.** Hold them accountable to solve their problems themselves.

Most often, this is uncomfortable. The other person will usually try the **VICTIM** or **PERSECUTOR** role to pressure you into backing down. Hang tough!

When my oldest son was about six years old, he wanted me to buy him a Nintendo video game system. It was brand new back then and cost about one hundred dollars. I said I would not buy it for him.

Certainly we could afford it and I love my children, so why wouldn't I buy it for him? Because then I would be stepping into the **RESCUER** role! He might not take care of it because it was my money that bought it; then I would get upset and go into the **VICTIM** role about how I provide all these things and he does not take care of them.

My son did a really good victim number: "Gee, Dad, I cannot afford to buy a Nintendo … I am only six."

What a **VICTIM**! His age was at fault and he could not help it. But I would not bite. I had played the game enough to know where this was headed, so I replied, "No, you can buy a Nintendo. I will help you buy it rather than buy it for you. How would you like to own your own business at age six?"

That sounded exciting to him.

I explained, "I will be your bank. Here is what you do. I will lend you the money to buy Christmas cards and you go around and knock on doors and sell the cards for six dollars a box. You get to keep one dollar for every box you sell and you give the five dollars back to me. That pays back the loan to me and makes me a little money for my risk if you do not sell enough boxes to pay the entire amount."

> To rescue is to insult, saying through your actions, "You are inca-

He went out and sold about two hundred boxes of Christmas cards. It was enough to buy not only the Nintendo, but also several of the game cartridges that went with it.

By choosing to act responsibly and by using my influence to help him act responsibly, we solved the problem without playing the game. And if he did not take care of his Nintendo, I would not get upset. It was his hard-earned money and time that created the Nintendo, not mine.

I managed to avoid the trap. Ten years later, however, he turned sixteen and wanted me to buy him a brand-new Jeep Cherokee. "I'm sixteen," he said, "and all the other parents are buying their kids cars."

I said that his age and the doubtful fact that all the other parents were doing it was not a good reason. I was not going to be the **RESCUER.**

He shifted to the **PERSECUTOR** role and attacked me with, "You talk in your seminars about giving. Now is the time to give to me. Practice what you preach."

I was not going to play the game. "Do you remember when I would not buy you a Nintendo when you were six?" I asked.

He did. I said, "This is the same thing. You are sixteen and totally capable of buying your own car. Get a job after school and save up."

"That will take forever," he complained.

I replied, "I understand, so we will do this. You go to work for at least three months and show me the pay stubs so I know you can hold a job. Based on the size of your pay stubs, we will know how much of a car payment you can handle. Then I will co-sign on a loan at a bank for you. You will build up credit and have your car. I will not make any payments. Should you miss payments

> How to solve the problem without playing the game: *HELP OTHERS SOLVE THEIR OWN PROBLEMS.*

and be in danger of losing the car, I will sell the car so my credit does not get ruined along with yours."

He agreed and went to work. After three months of employment, he showed me his pay stubs. (If I had not done that, he might have worked a week, gotten me to co-sign, and then quit his job. I would then be in the game as the **VICTIM**.)

I chose to be responsible, and so did he. Based on his pay stubs, he bought a used Ford Escort. Not quite what he wanted, but he had a car and he was learning about being responsible.

Be alert!

This game is played everywhere. Be alert. You might not catch it until you are in the game, but awareness is the first step to change. Then, every once in a while, you will manage to avoid the game. You will be responsible and cause the other person to be responsible.

The more you do this, the better you will get at it. Being a master at anything requires time and practice.

Increase your awareness of people who are playing the game, refuse to play, and choose to be responsible and help others be responsible as well.

Lesson #10

Finding the Real You

Who are you? **Have you ever really thought about that?**

This is one of the most important questions you can ever ask yourself.

Why? Because it determines much of your behavior. In fact, **who you believe yourself to be matters MORE than who you really are.**

We all view life through a set of paradigms or belief systems. I call these paradigms "sunglasses." (My book, *If How To's Were Enough*, goes into greater detail on this topic.)

The concept of "sunglasses" is simple enough:
> If you have a green pair of sunglasses and are looking at a white shirt, then the color you see or experience is green. If your glasses are pink, blue, or red, you will experience those respective colors. Whatever the color, the white shirt is not seen.

Obviously, the glasses you look through determine what you see or experience. If that is the case, then perception is *not reality* as some have claimed.

Instead, perception determines your experience.

To discover who you are, you must first discover who you are *NOT*.

Key #1: Are you your behavior?

Have you ever eaten peanut M&Ms? The peanut in the center is coated in chocolate, a thin layer of hard candy, and a colored shell. It looks something like this:

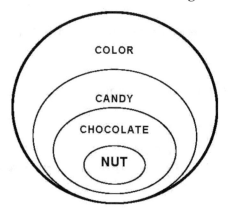

The way you view yourself is very similar, as the following diagram illustrates:

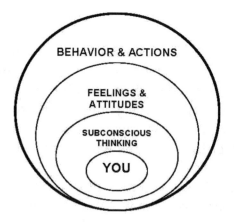

Are you your behavior? **How you answer this question will be a major factor in how you view yourself.**

Imagine you did something inappropriate as a child, like stealing a toy from a department store, and your Mom or Dad reacted by shouting, "You are bad, bad, bad!"

It would be easy to conclude, **"I did something bad ... therefore I am bad."**

As a result, you begin to define who you are based solely on your behavior. *You decide that you are your behavior.*

Viewing yourself through this set of glasses causes your self-esteem to fluctuate like a yo-yo. When you do manage to behave properly, your self-esteem rises, but when you behave badly, then your self-esteem plummets. Up and down you go!

As an adult, the trend continues. For example, if you get a raise at work, your self-esteem goes up, but if you have a bad month in sales, your self-esteem goes down.

To keep your self-esteem up, you have to work extremely hard to do the right thing *all the time*. Talk about a rat race!

The truth is, however:

YOU ARE NOT YOUR BEHAVIOR!

Your behavior is more like the color on an M&M or a jacket you wear when it is cold outside. You can take off the jacket or color—*the outer layer*—without affecting what is on the inside.

Clearly, it is absurd to think a jacket on the outside would define who you are on the inside, but a lot of people believe that their actions define who they are.

Not true! You are not your behavior. **You can even fail at something and still have high self-esteem because that particular failure does not define who you are.** You may have failed a test but you are not a failure.

It has nothing to do with the __real__ you. Your self-esteem is based on who you are, not on what you do.

Key #2: Are you your feelings?

Again, how you answer this question will determine the set of glasses through which you create your experience.

If you believe you are your feelings, then you will be afraid of any negative feelings. To be depressed or even 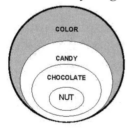 sad would indicate there was something wrong with you.

With an M&M, what is right underneath the outside color? It's the thin white layer of candy, right? And using the jacket analogy again, if the jacket represents your behavior, then your feelings would be the next layer or the equivalent of your shirt.

Are you your shirt? Of course not! Therefore, just as with behavior …

YOU ARE NOT YOUR FEELINGS!

Your feelings, which reside underneath your behavior and actions, **do not represent you.** When you understand this truth, you can have feelings like anger, sadness, or depression and still know you are okay! You are okay because the feelings have nothing to do with **WHO** you are!

Does this mean you do not always have to be happy? **Absolutely!** Do you have to always be up? **No!**

What a relief!

Key #3: Are You Your Thinking?

By now, you already know the answer. The answer is *NO!* Your thinking, especially your subconscious belief system, is simply one more level that you operate from, but you are not those beliefs.

Your subconscious thinking consists of sunglasses that create thoughts like:

- I am a loner.

- I am less than someone else.

- I am not worthy.

- I cannot trust people.

Or perhaps you have thoughts like:

- I am the greatest.

- I am a terrific athlete.

- I can trust people.

- I can accomplish my goals.

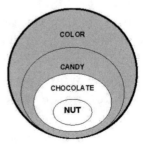

Whatever your thinking, whether good or bad:

YOU ARE NOT YOUR THINKING!

With your M&Ms, what is beneath the white candy? Chocolate, isn't it? This represents your subconscious thinking, and with the jacket analogy, it would represent whatever you wear under your shirt.

Either way, you are neither what you wear nor what you think.

Key #4: Who Are You?

What is at the very center of the peanut M&M? What is inside the chocolate? It is the nut, right? You are the nut in the middle! (Well, figuratively speaking anyway.)

In review, we have determined the following:

- **You are not your actions.**

- **You are not your feelings.**

- **You are not your thinking.**

But all of this merely says who you are __not__. I can tell you who I think I am, but that does little to help you. What you need is to arrive at your own conclusions as to who you are, **because who you think you are will determine your experience**.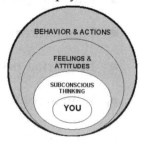

Have you ever noticed how each layer of the M&M is connected to the next layer? Sometimes it is hard to tell where one layer ends and the other begins.

It is the same with you! Your <u>behavior</u> and <u>feelings</u> and <u>thinking</u> are so closely connected that any time you change one, *you automatically affect all the others.*

For example, have you ever been told, "You need to change your attitude"?

We all have, but how often have you been told precisely HOW to change your attitude?

Why don't people tell you how to change your attitude? **Simply because they do not know how to change an attitude!** They just preach and tell you what to do.

If you have an argument with a family member, then go to a meeting with an important client, you had better change your attitude before you walk in that door! But practically speaking, how can you change an attitude?

Here's the key:

TO CHANGE YOUR ATTITUDE, CHANGE YOUR BEHAVIOR FIRST!

Imagine Sue and Mary are friends and love to dance. They call each other up every Friday night after work and make plans to go dancing. One Friday night, Sue calls Mary and says, "It's Friday night, so let's go dancing."

Now let's suppose Mary has had a really bad day: her boss yelled at her, she failed to complete a project, she got a speeding ticket, et cetera. If she responds as most people would, what would she say?

Quite likely, she would say, "No, I don't feel like it."

Notice her <u>feelings</u> determined her actions. Most people are totally victimized by their feelings. **Their feelings run their lives!**

If they do not feel well:

- They do not pick up the phone at work and prospect.

- They mistreat their families.

- They make poor management decisions.

Conversely, if they feel great:

- They pick up the phone and make the business call.

- They treat their families with kindness.

- They make better decisions.

Some will say you can control your feelings in order to control your behavior, but remember the key to changing your attitude is to change your behavior first. **The key to changing your attitude or feelings is to change your behavior first.**

What would happen if Sue responded to Mary's, "I don't feel like it" with, "Mary, I don't care how you feel, you should go dancing anyway"?

After a couple of hours of dancing, how does Mary feel? No doubt, she is feeling better. She changed her behavior (starting dancing instead of sitting on the couch) and now she feels better. **Her change in behavior changed her feelings and attitude.**

The Quick Solution

I have asked audiences to participate in a simple exercise where I ask them to rank how they feel on a scale of 1 to 10, where 10 equals "euphoric" and 1 equals "in the pits." (5 is about average.)

Next, I tell everyone that when I count to three, they should jump out of their chairs and yell, "I am excited!"

I admit it sounds ridiculous, but I challenge them to play my silly little game and see what happens. After jumping and screaming three times, I ask them to once again rate how they feel.

Almost without exception, everyone has a higher number. **They changed their behavior and changed their feelings.**

Those who do not have higher numbers usually admit that they really did not make an honest attempt to change their behavior. They barely got out of their chairs and were lukewarm in their response, thinking all the while, "This is really stupid." *No real change in behavior brought no real change in feelings.*

The Lasting Solution

There is only one problem with the results gained from the exercise I just described. *It provides no lasting benefit!*

In fact, some people *within a matter of seconds* revert back to the way they felt before they jumped up. Some take a few minutes, but the results usually do not last very long.

Why? Because the decision to jump up and scream is at the **outside** level (behavior and actions) and is therefore limited to only affecting the feelings and attitude level. As a result, the change is just temporary. This is why behavior modification usually does not work. It is an outside-in approach.

The way to create lasting results comes through exploring your subconscious thinking—*your belief systems*—and making changes at that level. This is more difficult, but the changes resulting from this approach are long lasting.

The reason for change

If you held an orange in your hand, and I asked you to squeeze it and you did, what would come out? Orange juice, of course. Why? For the obvious reason that orange juice is what is inside the orange.

Similarly, what is **inside** of you will come out when you are squeezed.

- Have you ever been squeezed by life?

- Have you ever been squeezed financially?

- Have you ever been squeezed or challenged in your marriage or as a parent?

- Have you ever been squeezed by having a health challenge?

What came out of you when you were squeezed? Were you satisfied with your response? Are there changes you need to make?

That is why we do character leadership/character development seminars. It works on the inside because it is always an inside job.

If so, that is why it is so important to work on yourself from the **inside**, dealing with your belief systems. Sooner or later you will be squeezed by life, and squeezed more than once!

Outside change, inside change, or both?

Even though working from the outer behavior and actions level does not produce lasting results, do not throw away that knowledge. It has its place, time, and usage. Remember the example earlier of having an argument at home and then walking into a meeting with an important client?

You need an immediate change! Run around your car or jump up and down.

> Changing your subconscious thinking (your belief systems) will not change you. It will change your results and the experience you are having in life.

Don't worry that your change is only temporary. Do whatever (ethically) works at that precise moment.

Herbert Horita at one time was the largest developer in the state of Hawaii. At one point, almost overnight, the

Japanese stock market plummeted and he lost all of his financing. Unfortunately, he was in the process of building major hotels, golf courses, and more! He suddenly was in very serious trouble.

How he responded to his challenges is what I found most interesting. Whenever he felt down or discouraged, he would go into his private office and do what he called his silent cheer. He would jump up and down, wave his arms, but make no noise. Remember, this was a multimillionaire, mature Japanese businessman!

Then he would go out and greet his executives. His change in behavior affected his feelings, which influenced how he interacted with his executives, impacted his decision making, and instilled confidence among his staff.

Did his positive feelings last after his silent cheer? No. *But doing so solved his immediate problem.*

The point is, a combination of **BOTH** an "inside out" and an "outside in" approach can be helpful in overcoming challenges you face.

The real you

You know or have learned the following:

- **You are not your behavior or how you act.** That's just what you do.

- **You are not your feelings.** You have feelings, but that's not who you are.

- **You are not your thinking.** You think, but that is not who you are.

So *WHO* are you? **What you decide will determine your experience.** I will give you my viewpoint, but you will have to make up your own mind. I believe:

YOU ARE A SPIRITUAL BEING.

You are a spirit with a body, feelings, and thoughts. For example, what kind of goals do you have? To lose weight, make more money, get in shape, et cetera.

How long-term are your goals?

> **Do you have written goals for the end of this year?** *In my experience, 70 percent of the population does not.*

> **Do you have five-year goals written out for your life?** *In my experience, 90 percent of the population does not.*

> **Do you have goals for five hundred years from now?**

You might be wondering, "Why would anyone have goals for five hundred years from now? We will not be here anyway!" The reason we do not think of setting such long-range goals is because **we think we are our bodies.** We think we are the physical bodies we have, and when the body dies, we think we die. In reality, only our bodies expire.

However, if you think of yourself as a spiritual being with a temporary body, then you will set goals for long after your body is buried in the ground. **That changes things, doesn't it?**

Most people in life are very short sighted. They are only concerned about how they feel at the moment. Instead, they should be concerned about how they will feel as a result of their actions one year, five years, or even twenty years down the road. In addition, what will others experience as a result of their actions after their bodies have left this earth?

In the 1960s, the "If it feels good, do it" approach to life got a lot of people into trouble, and I am not even talking from a moral point of view. I am speaking from a very practical point of view.

I encourage my children to look at things from a **"If it feels good tomorrow, do it today"** point of view. That is a spiritual, long-term approach.

For example, using illegal drugs or getting drunk might feel good to them at the moment, but it will not feel good tomorrow. Goofing off in school feels good at the moment, but it does not feel good when they experience fewer job opportunities tomorrow. Being a couch potato at the moment feels good, but feeling lethargic and depressed does not feel good tomorrow.

Sure, they might risk rejection from peers by choosing not to do drugs or get drunk, but being sober and alert feels good tomorrow. Studying hard in school and exercising will not necessarily feel good today, but tomorrow it will be worth it.

Most people are worried about the amount of their paycheck this week, but they should be more concerned about what their paycheck will be as a result of their actions one year or five years from now, or even after they are dead! After all, others they love and care about will continue to live on and be affected by their decisions.

When my children started to work, I encouraged them to not seek the highest paying job, but instead to seek the job they could learn the most from and the one that would set them up for years down the road. Thinking about what they wanted to do years from now and how a job contributed or detracted from that was more important than the immediate paycheck they would receive.

> If it feels good tomorrow, then do it today.

Similarly, most company leaders are very concerned about their immediate profits, but they should be concerned about their long-term profits. If they believe they are really spiritual beings, then they would be concerned about what will happen to the company long after they are no longer working there. They would be involved with the training and succession of others who will replace them.

If you believe you are a spiritual being who also has a body, then you are concerned with your legacy and how you are remembered. This does not mean you cannot enjoy life, but thinking about both the present and the future, even after your body is gone, will alter your approach to life and the decisions you make.

So, if you are not your behavior, not your feelings, not your thinking, and not your body, then who do **YOU** think you are ... **REALLY**? Shouldn't you think about that most important question?
After all, your conclusion will:

- Determine the stability of your self-esteem.

- Determine your view of life.

- Determine your level of satisfaction.

- Determine your response when squeezed by life.

- Determine your ability to set and accomplish goals.

Your total life experience will flow from what you decide!!

Changing from the outside in is easy, but it does not last.

Changing from the inside out is hard, but it does last.

To reach Brian Klemmer or Klemmer & Associates:

BY PHONE:
(707) 559-7722

TOLL FREE:
(800) 577-5447

BY FAX:
(707) 762-1685

BY U.S. MAIL:
1340 Commerce St, Suite G
Petaluma, CA 94954

By E-mail:
mastery@klemmer.com

Champions Workshop

The Champions Workshop is a 2-½ hour fun, impacting, and experiential workshop based on the "Formula of Champions." Brian Klemmer has interviewed Olympic world record holding athletes, CEOs of major corporations, and successful people of all walks of life in an effort to find the common denominators and keys to success. *The Formula of Champions is the result!*

Have you ever wanted something but were stuck because you didn't know what to do? *Never again! Here is a formula for producing results when you have no idea what to do. You can put this to use immediately.*

Is there a gap between what you want and what you actually get? *Learn why what you want has nothing to do with what you create.*

Present the attached perforated postcard and you can attend for FREE! This power-packed, riveting workshop is one of many workshops offered by Klemmer & Associates worldwide. Regularly $59.00!

If you need further information, call 800-577-5447 or visit www.klemmer.com.

Notes

Notes

Notes

Notes